Southport
&
Formby Memories

SOUTHPORT & FORMBY MEMORIES

The publishers would like to thank the following companies for their

support in the production of this book

R.W. Almond Builders Merchants Ltd

Cockshott Peck Lewis

Connards Jewellers

David Halsall Sons & Daughter Ltd

Demeva Ltd

K.A. Farr & Co

Hodge Halsall LLP

C.H.Latham

Millars Ark Toys Ltd

The Promenade Care Home

Silcock Leisure

First published in Great Britain by True North Books Limited
England HX3 6SN
01422 244555
www.truenorthbooks.com

ISBN 978 - 1906649715

Text, design and origination by True North Books
Printed and bound by The Amadeus Press

Southport
&
Formby Memories

CONTENTS

INTRODUCTION

Inside this book is a wealth of nostalgia, a sheer luxury of reminiscence. Page after page of memories will come flooding back to those of us who recall Southport and Formby as they were in the middle years of the last century. We can relive the days when we took rides from under the pier and along the beach in an amphibious DUKW or strolled through pine trees where red squirrels abounded on our way to the

century. There really was an age, not that long ago, when the car did not reign supreme and when children played happily with home made toys, without a computer chip in sight. A man lifted his hat when meeting a woman in the street. He also offered her a seat on the bus. Kiddies called teachers 'Sir' and 'Miss' and not by their Christian names. Bobbies appeared walking their beat or stood in the street directing vehicles on point duty. There

were markets that did not need the prefix of 'super' and places where goods were sold by the ounce and charged for in shillings and pence. If this strikes a chord, then this publication is the one for you.

So, prepare for a journey back in time to a land where the pace was much more gentle and that bit quieter. Why not get in the mood by relaxing in a comfy chair with a glass of dandelion and

dunes. This was when dad had a Ford Prefect in which he crammed the family to take us on a day out at the seaside. Further back than that, within these pages is a glimpse of the shops, transport and activities experienced by people from even earlier generations. The glorious photographs and thoughtful text that accompanies them helps pinpoint the changes in fashion, lifestyle and attitude that have occurred since late Victorian and Edwardian days.

Those of us who are native to the area know that Formby and Southport have separate histories and, indeed, identities. It is only since 1974 that they have been lumped together as part of Sefton. This book gives the reader an opportunity to get a real feel for those times that have become just a hazy memory for some and a mere piece of history to others. Just as the sand in the dunes is ever altering, so the nature of our district continues to evolve. A flavour of this can be seen by comparing the retail outlets of yesteryear on Lord Street with how they are today, and the face of a sleepy tree-lined Church Road with the one along which traffic now crawls.

Southport & Formby Memories is not a dry and dusty history book, but a celebration of life in the earlier decades of the last

burdock by your side. Pop an old 78 onto the gramophone, wind it up and listen to Edna Savage singing her version of 'Arrivederci Darling'. Open a packet of Spangles and you are ready to turn the first page.

Last, but by no means least we would like to thank a selection of Southport & Formby companies who have supported the production of this publication. Within these pages the story of each of them is told - their own proud histories and prospects for the future adding to the rich tapestry of the area....Happy reading!

TEXT	ANDREW MITCHELL, STEVE AINSWORTH, TONY LAX
PHOTOGRAPH RESEARCH	TONY LAX
DESIGNER	SEAMUS MOLLOY
BUSINESS DEVELOPMENT MANAGER	PETER PREST

Above: Horse-drawn carriages are evident in both of these photographs, as a means of transporting both people and goods. Directly behind the horse and cart in the picture above is the Opera House, built on Lord Street, first opened its doors to the people of Southport on 7 September 1891. It was designed by Frank Matcham, the pre-eminent architect of theatres in the UK. Matcham and two architects he helped to train, Bertie Crewe and W.G.R. Sprague, were together responsible for more than 200 of the theatres and variety palaces of the great building boom which took place in Britain between about 1890 and 1915. The Opera House seated 2,000 patrons, and cost around £20,000 to build! The theatre was considered to be one of Matcham's finest creations and was a great success until December 1929 when a fire raged through the building completely destroying it.

Right: This is as Parisienne an experience as you could get towards the end of the 19th century. Southport's Lord Street was as much a boulevard as any boasted by the French capital. Elegant shops with fashionably attired ladies patronising them were the order of the day. It is not just haute couture that provides a link across the Channel. Prince Louis Bonaparte, nephew of the famous Napoleon Bonaparte, lived on Lord Street from 1846 until becoming Emperor Napoleon III in 1851. Many argue that he helped design the wide streets in and around Paris as a result of his enjoyment of the grandeur he experienced in the layout of Lord Street. Whatever the truth, this is a fine and distinctive one mile stretch of a street not bettered anywhere in Britain.

SOUTHPORT STREET SCENES

Above: Leyland Arcade opened in October 1898, not long before this shopping scene was photographed. Even so, the bike stands could have been lifted from an image today as this sort of contraption still has its uses as many of us have turned back the clock and taken to two wheels as a favoured way of getting around. The arcade was designed by G E Bolshaw and had been eight years in the creation. Named after a local MP, Sir Herbert Leyland, it had been the brain child of John Humphrey Plummer. This entrepreneur had the idea of linking it all the way through from Lord Street to the Promenade. However, he fell out with the owner of an adjacent plot of land and had to be content with ending the arcade at West Street. Much of the wrought ironwork, glass and mahogany shop fronts are as they were well over a century ago. Along the left hand side we now have names such as Sweet Memories, Vintage Home, Rohan and Pudding and Pie opposite Mother and Child, Zapatoes and MultiYork. Even these suggest an old world charm and elegance. A statue of the celebrated Grand National winner Red Rum now accompanies diners down below, but Kate Greenaway's Café above is no more. The arcade was known as Burton's Arcade in the 1950s after the 'tailor of taste' purchased it. Since 1976 it has been called Wayfarers Arcade and is a listed building.

Above and below: Lord Street is shown in 1950 and over half a century earlier in this pair of photographs. In the Victorian scene, the Kardomah café provides some historical and sociological interest. It was one of a chain of coffee shops that was very popular across the country, especially up to and including the 1950s. Several of the more upmarket ones boasted their own string quartets offering a soothing background of music above the noise of the rattle of crockery. The Vey brothers opened their first Kardomah in Liverpool in 1844. They were tea dealers and grocers. The business was taken over by the Liverpool China and India Tea Company in 1868 and a Kardomah brand of tea was introduced in 1887. A particularly distinctive Kardomah café, designed by Misha Black, was built in Manchester in 1950. However, this was late in the day for such enterprises as jazz and pop music dominated coffee bars became the new rage as that decade developed. In the more modern photo, note the lack of road markings on the pedestrian crossing. The zebra markings did not become mandatory until 1951.

Top left and left: In these images of the late 19th century, Nevill Street was a thriving collection of shops and tearooms. The town had already become a popular place for visitors wanting to take the air and enjoy the fun and attractions that belonged to a better class of seaside resort. It was the advent of the railways that opened up the country for the working classes. People who had never travelled more than a few miles from their own homes suddenly discovered vistas on the far edges of their own county or even across on the other side of the country. Perversely, however, although the 'iron horse' brought visitors by the trainload, it was Southport's proximity to the canal system that gave it a head start over other northwest holiday spots. The Leeds-Liverpool canal was only a few miles away and William Sutton, a major influence in the town's early development, arranged transport links from the waterway to his bathing house at South Hawes and the neighbouring sandy dunes. In later years, people enjoying a cuppa in the Old Castle Tea Room on Nevill Street raised their mugs in Sutton's honour for giving them a chance to find a special holiday spot where they could forget the cares of the world for a while.

Above: An early picture of the Queen Victoria momument on an island site at the junction with the promenade. Sculptured by George Frampton, the 11.5ft statue was unveiled in the gardens opposite the library on Lord Street in July 1904. In December 1912, the sculpture was moved to Nevill Street where it remained until 2005. Victoria was monarch of the UK and Ireland from 1837 until her death in 1901. Her reign of 63 years and 7 months, is longer than that of any other British monarch and the longest of any female monarch in history. According to one of her biographers, Giles St Aubyn, Victoria wrote an average of 2,500 words a day during her adult life. From July 1832 until just before her death, she kept a detailed journal, which eventually encompassed 122 volumes. Today, standing on Nevill Street near the Promenade, a few yards from her original location, she forms part of a new civic area.

Looking northeast along tree-lined Lord Street from this elevated position, we get a fantastic snapshot of the times. During the 1920s automobile transportation was becoming much more affordable, however, in this picture the traffic was still relatively light, as most people preferred to use shanks's pony. As we travel along Lord Street we can see the impressive spires of Christ Church and St George's. The spire of Christ Church is no more to be seen, as this part was demolished in the 1950s when it became unsafe. This left the tower on its own, along with its three round windows that were originally intended to hold clock faces until funds ran out! Founded in 1821, the church soon became too small for a growing congregation and was replaced in 1865. Just over a century later, the structure was found to be unsafe and the building closed. A mixture of hard work, fund raising and prayer helped build a new church, attached to the old façade that opened in 1995. Further along, past the War Memorial, we can see St George's Presbyterian church, now United Reformed church. Founded in 1874, it was altered by Irving & Mosscrip, in 1931, and is now Grade II listed. Not to be outdone, in the centre background of the image we have the magnificent architecture of Holy Trinity Church at the junction of Hoghton Street and Manchester Road. This is the third church on this site since 1837 and is now grade II* listed.

These photographs show how the face of London Square was dramatically changed by the construction of the monument and memorial to those who fell in the Great War of 1914-18. In the earliest scene, dating from the early 1900s, the trams had come to town. They provided a quick, cheap source of public transport as they moved efficiently along the electrified tramway. They would provide a service until the last one completed a journey on New Year's Eve, 1934. The open topped trams acquired 'lids' from 1919 onwards and their dominance on the road was challenged by buses after the Corporation introduced its first Vulcan in 1924. This was a year after the 20-metre-high obelisk, commemorating the 1,273 who fell in the war, was unveiled. A national competition had been held to find an appropriate design that was both majestic and moving. Liverpool architects, Grayson and Barnish, were awarded the contract and the cost of £30,000 was raised by public subscription. The Cenotaph is flanked by a pair of pavilions, on whose Roman Doric colonnades the names of those killed in World War II have since been added.

Below and bottom right: Looking towards the railway station, with York Road to the left, the main structure in view is the imposing Birkdale Town Hall. Until it amalgamated with Southport in 1912, Birkdale was master of its own destiny. In 1902, Weld Road looked a bit of a mess, but traffic was light and early Edwardians were not too fussed about a few horse droppings and the occasional pothole. The Town Hall was built in 1871 and enlarged four years after this photograph was taken. This coincided with the creation

of the Carnegie Library to the right. The police courts stood just further on, having been completed in 1891. There was also a fire station on this site for a while. After the Town Hall lost its powers the premises were used by the Inland Revenue until 1962. This block of buildings has since been demolished and replaced by shops and offices. A taxi rank is now marked on the road where the cyclist is standing.

Above: Just a couple of cars can be seen on Liverpool Road in Birkdale in this 1920s picture. The vehicle on the left was turning into Bolton Road, just by the Liberal Club. The building looks very different now, having lost the top stage of its tower and the façade remodelled. It has also had alterations made to its political affiliation as it is currently the Labour Club. Ninety years ago, the Liberals were still a major force, though their pre-World War I dominance was waning significantly. Lloyd George was still prime minister at the start of the 1920s, but by the end of the decade Labour's J Ramsay MacDonald was in Downing Street.

Below: Rotten Row runs alongside Victoria Park. In the 19th century it was referred to as a 'very indifferent thoroughfare'. However, it was remodelled around the time that Birkdale UDC became part of the county borough of Southport in 1912. The delightful herbaceous border that stretches for over half a mile was created about that time. After World War One, Rotten Row became quite a fashionable parade where one could stroll or sit on a bench and just take in the joys of the plants and flowers that made it quite a genteel place to be. The name is thought to be a contraction of 'route de roi', translating as 'way of the king'. It would not have shamed royalty in its heyday as a team of 30 gardeners worked on it. Visitors came from far afield to enjoy the splendour and, in the 1930s, this landscaped area was a real tourist attraction. It became somewhat neglected towards the end of the last century, but Birkdale Civic Society obtained lottery funding and this cash, along with the fine efforts of volunteers, has helped restore many of the beds and borders to former glories.

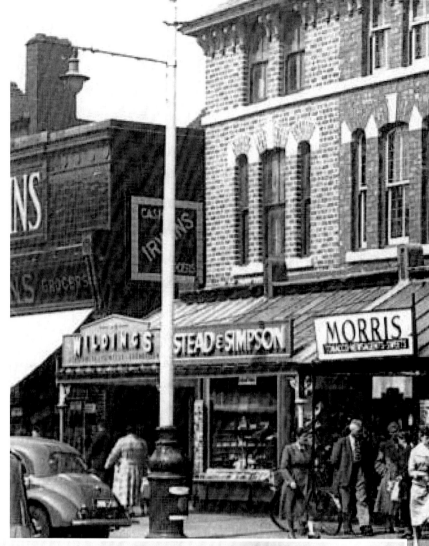

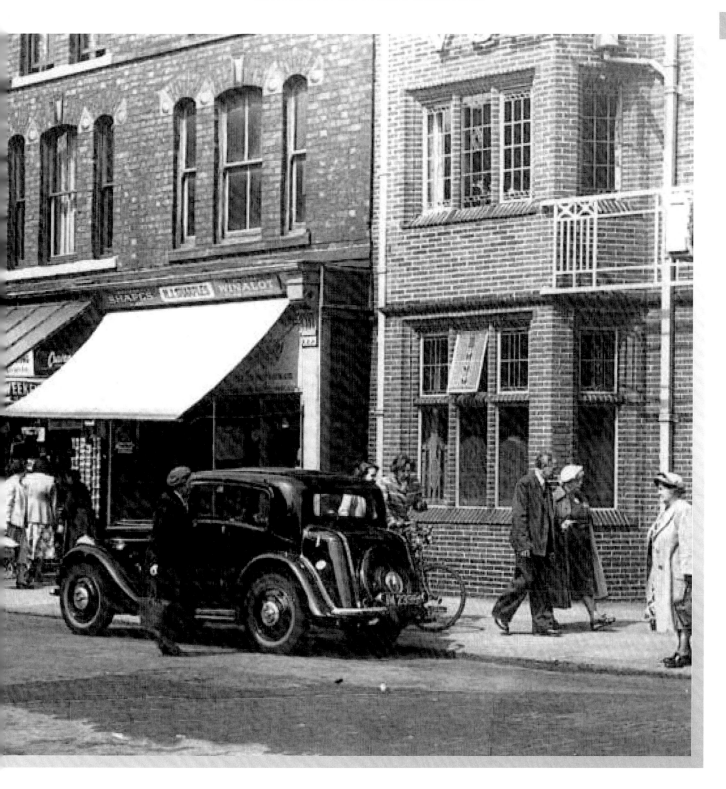

Above: Eastbank Street is now one of the main entry roads to Southport as it connects with the M58 motorway, providing quick access from the M6 and beyond. Such superfast highways were unheard of in Britain in the early 1950s. We were still recovering from the economic disaster that was one of the aftermaths of the Second World War. It was a period of belt tightening and austerity all round. Some parts of town have changed little over the years, but this row, opposite Princes Street, is much the same today as it was then. The parade of shops is still flanked by a pair of pubs, The Old Ship to the left and a Thwaites house, The Volunteer, to the right. The names on the shops may now include Rug Studio and Streets Ahead, the latter an Alder Hey Children's Hospital charity shop, but little else has altered. It is reassuring to know that we can still find little oases of yesteryear that have stayed with us.

Below: Looking the length of Nevill Street from its junction with Lord Street, the figure of Queen Victoria on her plinth on the edge of the Promenade can just be made out. Waterstone's book shop now occupies the large building on the left, with Jackpot Amusements just beyond. The corner site had long been home to the National and Provincial Bank that occupied the 1927 structure for many decades. Instead of lingerie, the store on the opposite corner now sells shoes and handbags and is owned by Russell and Bromley. Just look at all the cars parked up bumper to bumper. Traffic density was an issue in the 1950s, never mind in the current millennium.

Right: It is remarkable to think that there is half a nation out there that does not recall using shillings and pence on a daily basis. It is now over 40 years since our currency was decimalised and the words 'tanner', half crown' and 'florin' disappeared from our vocabulary. The prices in the grocer's shop window from the early days of the 20th century will need an Enigma machine to help younger readers decipher the cost of goods in Cooper's shop window. Tea at 1/6 per lb becomes one shilling and sixpence a pound. In other words, to the metric

monkeys, this is about 7.5p for each 450 grams. Cooper's was obviously keen on promoting Eiffel Tower goods, with its adverts for such diverse products as lemonade and baking flour. These lines were produced by Foster Clark of Maidstone, a company founded by George Foster Clark in 1891 after culinary experiments in his mother's kitchen. The firm is still in business today, though, after various acquisitions, its base is in Malta.

Bottom right: The Co-op building, on the corner of Eastbank Street and Kings Street, boasts something of an art deco look. It was built in 1934 to a design by Cropper and Johnson. The latter was the Co-op's senior planner and the former had travelled in Russia looking for inspirational architectural ideas. The rounded part of this branch held the stair well and the butchery department was to its right. In 1950 the business was flourishing, despite austere times. The whole Co-operative business had come a long way since its humble origins in the Pioneers movement grocer's shop in Toad Lane, Rochdale. Now it was trading in all sorts of commodities that included travel, insurance and finance. In the middle of the last century, housewives still looked to this enterprise for a bit of 'divvi', a

form of loyalty shopping reward that pre-dated green stamps and the likes of Nectar cards. Towards the end of its time in this form of business, it became part of the Lancastria Co-op that also had large stores in Lancaster, Blackpool and Preston. Nowadays, it is used by McDonald's as a fast food eatery and also offers accommodation to Poundstretcher, a 'value' chain store.

In this1969 aerial view the outstanding feature is the magnificent architecture of Holy Trinity Church, at the junction of Hoghton Street and Manchester Road. This is the third church on the site since 1837 and is now grade II* listed. To provide the third church a scheme commenced in 1897 and was brought to a successful conclusion just over a year before the outbreak of the First World War. At the time the achievement was noted 'as a great witness to faith and generosity'. Running parallel to Hoghton Street is Southport's main thoroughfare, Lord Street, which can be seen middle left of picture, running between the two sets of tower blocks. The larger of the two buildings is Sandown Court, in Albert Road, whilst the other is Regents Court, a ten-storey block at the corner of Lord Street and Manchester Road. Further along the road is Southport's seat of justice, the law courts, which used to occupy the same building as the town's fire brigade and police headquarters. In the 1920s this area was taken up by Southport Municipal Secondary School for Boys, which originally occupied a building named 'The Woodlands', along with some disused Army huts. Looking to the left centre of shot is the flat roof of the former Grand Cinema which opened in 1938 and has since been home to the Grand Casino and Bingo Club and more recently Mint Casino.

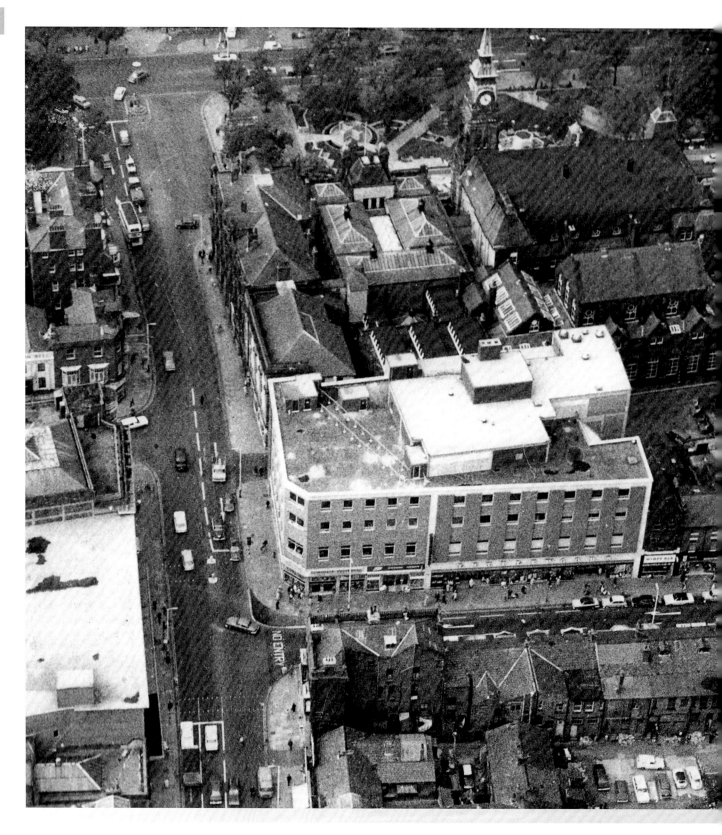

A fabulous elevated view of two of Southport's busiest shopping thoroughfares. Local Sandgrounder's will recognise that to the left is Eastbank Street and across the centre of the picture is Chapel Street. Evident in this image from the late 1960s we can clearly see three of the town's largest stores, Littlewoods, Broadbents and Marks & Spencer. The under-cover shopping centre of the Cambridge Arcade can also be identified next to Broadbents. What you wouldn't see today are cars parked along Chapel

© Stephenson Newspapers Ltd/Trinity Mirror North West

Street, which at the time was one way traffic leading out on to Eastbank Street, passing Lordsdale Universal on the corner. Today, Chapel Street has been transformed from a street dominated by busy traffic to a fully pedestrianised area, with trees, seating and plenty of space, providing better access for pedestrians to the shops and the railway station, which is off to the right of this photograph. Chapel Street is now one of Southport's retail hot spots and home to some of the UK's most recognised brands.

FORMBY
STREET SCENES

Formby may have developed into a small town in latter years, but for much of its early existence this was just a small hamlet or village. Even so, during its growth there were several noteworthy features that put it firmly onto the British map. Just over 1,000 years ago, Norsemen were attracted to invade the area from a base in Ireland. 'Formby' has Viking roots, as demonstrated in the name 'Fornebu', once the site of Oslo's airport. Formby Hall, now part of a golf course, has connections with the 13th century and it was as far back as 1776 that the country's very first lifeboat station was founded on the beach. It remained operational until the First World War. The small RAF airfield on the outskirts of town also has a claim to fame, as it was from there that the last operational flight of the legendary Spitfire took place in 1957. The main population growth took place in the first half of the last century and the building of the A565 bypass helped keep the town a quieter place than some of its neighbours. An attractive place to set up home, it has attracted local soccer stars such as Steven Gerrard and Alan Stubbs here at different times. Music hall entertainer George Formby adopted the town's name instead of his given one of Booth for his stage act, passing it on to his even more famous son in later years. Red squirrels, toads, forest and miles of sand dunes complete the picture for this delightful section of the Lancashire coastline.

Above: A misty view towards the town suggests a time in the early years of the last century when carts and not cars dominated. The garden shed and not the garage was to be found to the rear of dwellings in an era that was more rural than industrial. Factory chimneys and the like never came to this part of Lancashire. It was just the workforce from those mills inland and further east who ventured into our neck of the woods.

Top right, facing page: There is now a mixture of bungalows, semis and detached private residences along Kenyon's Lane, a street that runs east off Church Road. J Kelly's boot making business occupied part of the row of cottages in the days when working men needed sturdy footwear that would last. When soles and heels wore out, they got them repaired. They did not just go out and buy a new pair as we do today. This was a mend-and-make-do society long before the phrase was dreamed up in the 1940s. Mr Kelly lived in and worked out of his home in what was literally a cottage business. This part of Lancashire had strong Catholic traditions. The church in the background is that of Our Lady of Compassion on School Lane. It was consecrated

in 1864, fittingly on 14 August, the feast of the Assumption.

Right: St Peter's is an Anglican church on Green Lane, in the northwest quarter of the town. A former chapel of the same name once stood near the sea on the site now used by St Luke's, but that St Peter's was destroyed in a storm in 1739. A levy on congregations across the country helped provide funding for the new church that was built further inland. Major alterations took place in the 1870s, giving it much of the look it has today.

Below: The war memorial at Cross Green still stands on this roundabout, though it is a much busier scene today as it is surrounded by traffic turning into Three Tuns Lane, Duke Street and Liverpool Road that all meet here. Close by are a small supermarket and the handsome Cross House Inn that add to the hustle and bustle. Happily, the garden area in which the memorial stands is well tended and an appropriate backdrop to the sculpture by Keeley and Sons that was unveiled in November 1922 to honour those who fell in the 1914-18 War. Constructed from the finest Cornish granite, the wheel portion of the cross is fine axed and interlaced with runic carving that forms the Cross of St. George in the centre.

Formby has two railway stations, the first being Formby railway station and the second less than a mile north, Freshfield railway station. Formby station opened in 1848 and Freshfield opened six years later, in 1854. Both are on the Northern Line of the Merseyrail network, which runs from Liverpool to Southport. The importance of the railways in shaping the nature of the British countryside cannot be emphasised too strongly. Until the middle of the 19th century, very few people ventured far from the places where they were born and raised. Whether it was for the purpose of work or play, only those with ample funds indulged in meaningful travel. Even then, it was something of an

expedition involving much upheaval and journeys that were lengthy in terms of both time and distance. The speed and convenience of rail travel changed all that. Within a generation, families that had been based in a town or village for centuries suddenly fragmented and went off to seek employment and their fortunes all over the country. Changes in social status, though, were harder to come by, as we can see from the signs on the platform. There were three classes of rail ticket for the upper, middle and lower classes. Remarkably, that separation was continued into the designation of smoking areas so that toffs did not have to mix with the plebs.

Right: The horse droppings on Green Lane are a reminder of how important that noble beast was to our ancestors. They had no motorised transport and relied heavily on our four-legged friends for assistance in ploughing fields and pulling carts and carriages. The tower belongs to St Peter's Church. Two members of the Formby family from Formby Hall were incumbents of the church in the 19th century. It was during this period that restoration and remodelling work took place when the present chancel, sanctuary and side chapel were added.

Left: Gores Lane is in the north of town, not far from the golf club. It is still a pretty, tree-lined road that, despite being almost entirely residential, is a comparatively peaceful part of the area. There is even the occasional thatched property still to be found, providing more than just a passing link with this image of almost a century ago when the motor car was still something of a novelty. It was also seen as a bit of a nuisance to these people out for a spot of exercise as their stroll along one of Formby's attractive avenues was invaded by noise and fumes.

Above: Raven Meols Lane runs between Liverpool Road and Andrews Lane. The gas lamps on the street provide a delightful period feel to this image. The mother and child out for a walk would have approved of the way in which the roadway was illuminated in the evenings. These were dark and dangerous places before the advent of street lighting. The earliest ones required a lamplighter to tour the town at dusk, but later models had an automatic ignition system that went into action when the gas flow was started. It was not until the 20th century that electric lamps became the norm.

Left: These sweet little girls were safe enough, standing in the middle of Timms Lane. Clearly the girl on the right has something interesting in the palm of her left hand that she is keen to show it to the other little girl. The pace of life was so much gentler when the horse and cart rattled along the highways and byways. Children were expected to entertain themselves. There was no money for expensive toys, and the adults were too busy to help set anything up. We expected nothing else and we enjoyed ourselves. Fortunately there was little or no traffic, so the street was our playground: the roads, the pavements, and the tiny front gardens. The nasty boys would climb trees, play cricket or marbles whilst the girls would skip, play with a hoop or perhaps a game of hide and seek.

Below: This family, all dressed up in their Sunday best, could well have been about to worship at the new Methodist Chapel that opened on Elbow Lane at the turn into the 20th century. Back then, it was quite common practice to spend the morning of the Sabbath at church or chapel. The remainder of the day was also set aside as a period of rest and, for some, further contemplation. To even consider an outing to a music hall or variety theatre was frowned upon and decidedly off limits for supporters of the Lord's Day Observance Society.

The pair of photographs of Liverpool Road show how we used to find it much easier to enjoy ourselves before the hurly burly of modern society came our way. We were afforded the time to be children, rather than young adults. We were given opportunities to play and learn for ourselves what it was that was safe and that which made us sorry. Of course, we had little in the way of speeding cars to disturb our play, so we were able to mess about with

wheelbarrow rides. There was also that really pleasant pastime of just lounging about and taking it easy. When we look at the top right picture of the butcher's owned by Richard Rimmer, on the corner of Three Tuns Lane and Chapel Lane, there is a chance to reminisce about hares and rabbits hanging on meat hooks outside the shop and large hams and sides of bacon indoors, swinging from the ceiling above a sawdust sprinkled floor. Blood spattered aprons and a cheery, 'Nice bit of cowheel

and tripe, my love?' completed the scene. Lloyds Bank stands here now. The images of Chapel Lane include a view of the old post office, framed in a lovely period setting. It has some overtones of Dorcas's establishment in 'Lark Rise to Candleford' and you can just imagine a mixture of homespun philosophy being despatched along with the stamps. In those days there was only one class of post, namely first class. The street scene from the 1950s shows part of Formby's main retail area. Known locally as The Village, Chapel Lane and Brows Lane have got busier still in the intervening years as they reinforce their reputation as the town's premier shopping location.

Above: Trippers and locals alike came down Victoria Road, generally known here as Shore Road, from the direction of Freshfield Station. They kept a sharp lookout for those notoriously shy red squirrels as they made their way to the sands at the other end of the pine forest. The dunes made a natural wind break on draughty days as we lounged on the edge of the beach. Just after the war we also kept a wary eye for unexploded mines that were occasionally washed up on the shoreline. These woods are now home to one of the few thriving populations of Red Squirrels in Britain today. The area is also an important site for Natterjack Toads which inhabit the dunes. A nationally endangered species, protected by law. Natterjacks are distinguished from Common Toads by the yellow stripe down their back and yellow eyes.

Below: An unusual sight as a herd of cows amble along Duke Street, near Formby Bridge and the station. Close your eyes and you can almost imagine Frankie Laine belting out the theme song to 'Rawhide'. That was the early 1960s' TV series that kept us glued to our sets as we followed the exploits of a fictional cattle drive, set in the United States of the 1860s. It introduced a young Clint Eastwood into our homes as Rowdy Yates. The cows, though, were making a much shorter and less arduous journey.

Facing page: Sited on Green Lane, the Grapes Hotel is a well-established hostelry. A century ago the Grapes was the meeting place of the first pioneer aviators. Its position on the corner with Church Road, Piercefield Road and Ryeground Lane meant that it was always a magnet for passing trade as well as those locals who made it their own. These photographs trace the way the hotel looked from late Victorian times until the

middle of the 20th century. It would appear to have differed little from the original building that first saw the light of day in 1880. The structure included assembly rooms and there was also an outdoor bowling green for those who enjoyed a little bit more exercise than just lifting a glass to their lips. Polite society also enjoyed taking tea in one of the hotel's handsomely decorated rooms. An adjacent building on Ryeground Lane acted as its brewhouse. Across from the Grapes was a corner group of shops, which included a grocers, a fishmongers, a tobacconist and a few door down a baker. No need for a supermarket in those days with fresh bread, fish and butter from a wooden keg, readily available on your doorstep. Readers may also remember that across on the opposite corner of Piercefield Road which was once home to the Embassy Cinema. In modern times the Grapes has developed a reputation as a pub and restaurant, with a clientele that has included famous footballers and racegoers taking in Grand National week at Aintree. The façade and interior have been greatly altered in more recent times, but the links with the past remain in its history.

ALONG THE
PROMENADE

The Lower Promenade, as it was in the mid 1930s and late Victorian and Edwardian eras, is still popular today with visitors and locals both enjoying a stroll along here. Southport's Victorian entrepreneurs sought to develop the town as a better class of resort and aimed to attract a more upmarket clientele than its competitors. Although sideshows, fairs and amusement stalls would have their place, those who held the civic reins wanted to develop the seafront as a place that could also offer tranquil gardens, the waters and an opportunity for more sedate activities. The Marine Gardens were built and the Marine Lake constructed, opening on 7 September 1887. A torchlight procession, accompanied by a firework display, marked the occasion. Unfortunately, it was not long before it was realised that the lake sides were becoming eroded and a concrete edge had to be provided to prevent further deterioration. The first part of the lake had been built to the south of the pier and a northern section was added and joined on in 1895. Toilets and shelters were added to the Lower Promenade in the early 1900s.

Above, below and top right: Southport Pier is the second longest pier in Britain, after Southend Pier. It was first opened in 1860 with an original length of 3,600 ft and was further extended to 4,380ft in 1868. Designed by Sir James Brunlees, the pier took a year to build and was constructed on iron supports. Once completed the local people of Southport were treated to an opening celebration that was to go down into the history books. The pier was an instant hit, but it was no fun for newly arrived tourists humping heavy baggage along the full length to the pier head. A decision was made to erect a tram line, initially for luggage only but later to carry luggage and passengers. The tram line was first opened and put into use in 1862 and over the next few years the tram was upgraded to a steam powered tram. The tramway was re-laid in 1893 and electrified on April 3, 1905. Southport Corporation took over in 1936, and rebuilt the tramway's rolling stock. When the town

lost its DC electricity supply in 1950, the tramway's 3 foot 6 inches gauge line was replaced with one foot eleven and a half inches gauge using diesel stock. Southport pier has had several setbacks in its history, suffering at the hands of such disasters as fire, storms and boating accidents. In 1889 the refreshment rooms that had provided much needed rest and relaxation at the pier head collapsed following a storm which swept away the foundations. Maybe the biggest challenge, however, to the Grade II listed structure came when a demolition proposal was rejected by Sefton's Leisure Services Committee, by only one vote. Now under the Southport Pier Trust sufficient funding has been granted to totally redevelop the pier with additional financing from the Heritage Lottery Fund and the European Merseyside Objective. A trip to the English seaside wouldn't be the same without the opportunity to sample the delights of fish and chips, ice cream and candy floss, all in abundance along the pier. .

Below: Sir James Brunlees was the engineer who was the mastermind behind Southport Pier. It is thought to be the first leisure one in the United Kingdom. Waiting and refreshment rooms were added for boat passengers in 1862 and a cable operated tramway was included in 1865. Storm damage and fires in 1933 and 1957 reduced its length back to the original distance, but it is still Britain's second longest. Funland is still a major amusements attraction today. It

is owned by Silcocks, a family business that has its own history steeped in the fairground trade. This dates back to the 1880s when Edward Silcock founded his travelling fair that toured the north of England. At first, it contained little more than his 'Flyer', a coconut shy, a few simple rides and a handful of stalls. Success was swift and soon Silcock's four sons found employment with their father, developing the company into a household name.

Below: The Promenade was actually built in 1834, so visitors were walking the walk, as it were, even before Queen Victoria acceded to the throne. However, it was during her time as our monarch that the seafront here was developed as a major tourist attraction. She would have been about to hand over the regal reins to Edward VII when these promenaders hove into view. As we can see, the South Marine Gardens attracted large numbers, all anxious to enjoy the fresh air and beautiful environment of this delightful place. The only drawback was its very attractiveness as large crowds, especially at weekends, were drawn here. It became quite difficult to grab a quiet moment or secluded spot. These gardens opened in the year of the Queen's golden jubilee and soon they became the place for smartly dressed, middle class folk to be seen out and about. The men looked very dapper and the younger ladies wore the most fashionable of outfits. Even the children were in their Sunday best, though it is noticeable that an elderly woman in the centre is almost like Victoria herself; dressed from head to toe in widow's weeds.

Above and below: In the photograph below we are looking along the bridge across the Marine Lake. Just how many courting couples have made their way from one side to the other over the years is impossible to determine. Many a time you can spot more senior duos revisiting the moments from their youth when they strolled hand in hand over the water. Blackpool was where they went for fun and noise; Southport was the place for tranquillity and romance. In the scene from the accompanying image, the light coloured buildings in the right foreground are situated at the entrance to the pier. Beyond there and the rowers pulling on their oars, we can see the open air swimming baths on the far side of the lake. Further on are Noah's Ark and the big dipper belonging to the funfair.

The miniature railway that runs along the edge of the Marine Lake is typical of scores of these attractions that appeared in the early 20th century. Their popularity with youngsters, as well as those whom we will describe as 'young at heart', has seldom waned over the last century and more. Originally, the track was a straight line on the seaward side, with a loop at either end for use as a turning circle. The first journey was made on 25 May, 1911. It was then known by the name of its builder and operator, Mr G V Llewellyn. In 1918, the track was extended

to turn under the pier and into Marine Parade Station. It was further altered in 1938 and the line then, as now, measured about a mile in length. The first pair of steam locos, with a 4-4-2 design, were Bassett-Lowke Class 10 Atlantics. Named King George and Princess Elizabeth, these machines provided good service for a number of years before being supplanted by sturdier models. Now known as the Lakeside Miniature Railway, it is the world's longest running 15 inch gauge railway to be in continuous service.

Above: A fantastic picture, taken on a sunny day looking along Southport promenade towards the Floral Hall building. Mass crowds sit in deckchairs in the Floral Hall gardens, listening to relaxing music in front ot the bandstand. Judging by the vehicles parked at the roadside and the clothing being worn by the passers by, the image was probably taken in the mid-1960s. The Floral Hall building dates from the 1930s and is a flat-roofed brick building on classical lines, that still today retains the original art deco features. The Southport Theatre was added to the complex in 1973. Famous names such as

The Beatles have appeared live at the Floral Hall. Between 1962/63 the Beatles played four times, with the last performance being on 15 October, 1963. It took place on the day it was announced that The Beatles had been invited to appear on the Royal Command Performance and followed the group's appearance on Sunday Night At The London Palladium. 'Beatlemania' was about to grip the nation. Today, the Complex is multi-purpose and has benefited from a superb £3 million refurbishment programme. It is also home to the 4-star Ramada Plaza hotel.

Below: The handsome King's Gardens are home to delightful lawns, flower beds, walkways and the popular miniature railway and model village. They provide a lovely accompaniment to the Promenade and its large boating lake. Trippers and holidaymakers are torn between spending time here, along the pier or on the golden sands below. Seen in a collection of views

from the decades either side of the last war, the Gardens were opened by King George V in 1913. The earliest image shows the stretch heading southwest from Nevill Street towards the corner at Coronation Walk. This latter place can be seen at the traffic island, close to the Royal Clifton Hotel, now part of the Best Western group. Overleaf: the large double page spread following shows Queen Victoria incongruously gazing across to Funland. Her statue was designed by Sir George Frampton RA and was originally placed in 1903 in front of Cambridge Hall, Lord Street. It was the sculptor himself who requested the move to a more elevated position at the end of Nevill Street.

A stunning view along the Prom from the 1950s

EVENTS & OCCASIONS

Above: The Scarisbrick and Hesketh families owned much of the town's immediate foreshore in the late 19th century and agreed its sale to the Corporation in 1885 for a sum of just over £10,000. There was a proviso that any buildings erected on the seaward side of the Promenade would be solely for recreational use. Work on creating the first stage of the Marine Lake, south of the pier, was begun almost immediately. This was completed by 1887 and attention turned to completing the north section. Work was well under way by the turn into the next decade when a crowd gathered nearby to view the arrival of the barque, 'William Fisher'. This sailing ship was brought by the Corporation to lie off the beach as a tourist attraction. Built in Liverpool in 1844, it was a large merchant vessel crewed by 250

sailors. North Marine Lake and its complementary gardens were opened to the general public in 1892. The lake was further extended in the mid 1960s.

Right: As war erupted across Europe, men answered the call to arms. Starting with a force of less than 250,000 regulars, the British Army would absorb over five million men by 1918. The war would eventually touch almost every family in the country. Rudyard Kipling had long prophesised the war with Germany. He proclaimed "We must demand that every fit young man come forward to enlist and that every young man who chooses to remain at home be shunned by his community". He is seen here in Southport, at a rally to appeal for additional recruits.

Kipling is front centre, with the Mayor of Southport on the left in volunteer uniform. Joseph Rudyard Kipling was born in Bombay in 1865 and was taken by his family to England when he was five years old. He is best known for his works of fiction, including The Jungle Book, and his poems. Kipling received the 1907 Nobel Prize for Literature.

Above: If you think that bungee jumping from bridges or tombstoning off cliffs are dangerous, then what about this daredevil? At the turn into the 20th century, the self styled Professor Osbourne thrilled crowds with his diving feats. His leaps from a gantry or the roof of Tom's tearoom on Southport Pier brought gasps from the crowd. During the interwar years, other men emulated his feats. They included 'Peggy' Gadsby and Barney Pykett who were both one legged performers, having suffered injuries in the trenches during World War I. A sad footnote to their exploits is that they had to put their lives on the line again to earn a living, having already risked all in the service of their country.

On something akin to a wing and a prayer, the pilot took to the skies. Thousands packed the front to witness a display by the technological marvel of the age. It was only in the first decade of the last century that powered flight had become possible. The advancement was swift and soon Blériot was hopping over the Channel and shows like this one were being staged over the heads of large crowds. The sands and streets below this biplane have also played host to the motor racing world. The Southport Motor Club, inaugurated in 1902, attracted many famous drivers to the events it arranged. This was in the days before even the mighty

Brooklands circuit was created. A racecourse, roughly a mile in length, was created along the Promenade, with the Rotten Row slope used to enable deceleration and stopping to take place. Later, a circuit was created that included Lord Street, starting and finishing at the Convalescent Hospital. Our town boasted its own street race before Monaco, Detroit and the rest thought of it. Locals and dignitaries, though, objected to the closure of the town centre streets and racing was transferred to the beaches at Birkdale and Ainsdale. Henry Segrave set the world land speed record of

152 mph here in March 1926 and Malcolm Campbell competed on the sands in 1928 in a 100 mile race that attracted a crowd of 100,000.

Right: Mother Nature demands our respect and nowhere more so than in her seas. Time and tide, as they say, wait for no man and the latter had no intention of hanging around on this occasion in the late 1920s. A group of men had been cut off by the tide off the Marine Lake, not far from the old Convalescent Home, later to become the Promenade Hospital. Members of the police force and rescue services put their own lives in danger to get these careless folk to safety. Despite repeated warnings, people continue to take foolish risks even today. It was as recent as 2004 that 21 Chinese cocklers were drowned in Morecambe Bay and, in 2011, the RNLI lifeguards patrolling the beaches at Formby, Crosby and Southport cleared more than 9,000 people off sand banks over a four day period to stop them getting marooned. They also helped reunite 12 lost children with their parents.

Above: If you can resist saying 'Orrr' when you look at this image then your heart must be the hardest ever produced. What little loves they all are. The Rose Queen Festival was just one of thousands that took place every year up and down this green and pleasant land early in the last century. It is the sort of idyllic scene that makes TV programmes such as 'Lark Rise to Candleford', 'Downton Abbey' and 'Darling Buds of May' popular as we hanker back to days gone by that are now between 60 and 120 years in the past. Crossens is the most northerly of Southport's districts and it crowned its first Rose Queen in 1906. The festival was an annual event, except for two years during World War I, until 1964. As with so many quintessentially British customs, the tradition was then abandoned, being deemed out of date. How sad. Marvellously, it was revived in 1986 when the previous Queen, Liz Highton, née Leaf, crowned the new one. A procession around the village was held, followed by maypole dancing.

Left: A large crowd had gathered to witness the opening of the magnificent new sea-bathing pool on 17 May, 1928. A young swimmer is shaking hands with Lord Derby just after the ribbon cutting ceremony at the pool in Southport. The Mayor stands beside him and a large crowd sit in the spectator stand at the open-air pool. The girls, some with bouquets of white flowers, are champion junior swimmers from local schools, chosen to take part in the ceremony. The vest and shorts outfit with a belt were all the rage at that time. Other girls paraded round the side of the pool in bathing costumes and carrying parasols. Edward George Villiers Stanley, 17th Earl of Derby (4 April, 1865 – 4 February, 1948), known as Lord Stanley from 1893 to 1908, was a British soldier, Conservative politician, diplomat and racehorse owner. He was Lord Mayor of Liverpool between 1911 and 1912.

Above and right: Southport sits at the very centre of England's golf coast in the North West. Some of the UK's finest golf courses are here along the Wirral, Lancashire and Mersey coastline inclusive of three famous Royals - Royal Birkdale, Royal Liverpool and Royal Lytham & St Annes. Many of the courses around the Royals on the North West Golf Coast play host to major golf competitions such as the Ryder Cup and other amateur events. The Ryder Cup has been at Southport & Ainsdale and Royal Birkdale twice. In 1933 Southport & Ainsdale Golf Club hosted the Ryder Cup and British golf enthusiasts could not have dreamed that this exciting 6 to 5 victory would be our last Ryder Cup triumph for 24 years. In the final singles matches over 15,000 spectators eagerly followed the action. Seen here, A.G Havers of team GB has a tricky shot approaching the home green in his match with L. Diegel, whom he beat by 4 and 3. In 1933 The Prince of Wales was extremely popular, now here was he at the Southport & Ainsdale Golf Club in his capacity as President of the Professional Golfers Association to present the Ryder Cup to Great Britain. Making a reply is Walter Hagen, the U.S.A. captain, who thanked his Royal Highness for being at Southport & Ainsdale. Though the Ryder Cup would be staying in Britain they would not be downhearted. Mr Hagen closed by congratulating the Great Britain team on their excellent golf. On accepting the Trophy, J.H. Taylor, pictured left, the non-playing captain of the Great Britain team, said he was the proudest man in the British Commonwealth of people at that moment.

Above: In November 1914 the war was just a few months old. Mayor Henry Ball paid a visit to troops billeted in the town in a morale boosting exercise. At this time, men were heading off to France and Belgium singing 'Pack up your troubles' and expecting to return with their kitbags by Christmas as victory against 'the Hun' was just a formality. Yet, word filtering back from across the Channel suggested that our leaders had been overly optimistic in predicting swift success for the British Expeditionary Force. A bloody setback at Mons, a terrible defeat for the Russians at Tannenberg and stalemate in muddy trenches that already stretched from the North Sea to Switzerland did not bode well. A further four years of horror stretched ahead.

Massive crowds gathered on the streets to get a glimpse of their Majesties King George V and Queen Mary, on a brief visit to Southport. The stop-off in Southport, to open the newly created Kings Gardens, was part of an incredible week-long, 30-towns tour undertaken by the royal couple in July 1913. Part of the tour also included opening Gladstone Dock in Liverpool. It had been quite a stressful time for the Royal couple as the date would be remembered for more tragic reasons. A month earlier, during the 1913 Epsom Derby, Emily Wilding Davison, a women's suffrage activist, stepped in front of the King's horse Anmer, sustaining injuries that resulted in her death four days later. In Southport however, the mood was upbeat. Following the King and Queen's visit, fun and merriment took place on the water with a regatta and a carnival held on Marine Lake. The evening saw the lake and parks lit up with fairy lights and lanterns, which complemented illuminated boats on the water. Appropriately, for such an occasion, the evening ended with a firework display. In the picture left the King is seen talking to the Chief Constable.

Above: The open air bathing pool opened in 1914 amid some consternation from maiden aunts and churchmen who decreed that mixed dipping and all that flesh on display was not good for the soul. It served the resort until the larger sea bathing lake was created in 1928. Peter Pan's Pool and Playground took over the original site in 1930. The new lido measured 110 by 70 yards and held an astounding 1.4 million gallons of water. As we can tell from this crowded scene, this was a very popular place to be on a warm, summer's day. A budding Johnny Weissmuller or Esther Williams could show off aquatic skills to anyone who cared to watch. There are still many lidos and open air pools in existence in Britain today, but ours was lost to the resort when it closed in 1989 and was demolished not long afterwards. It is sad that such an iconic part of our town's history has fallen by the wayside, but at least we have our memories to sustain us.

© Southport Visitor/Trinity Mirror North West

Left and above: In the years after World War II, beauty contests were being introduced in a number of seaside resorts around Britain. Towns like Eastbourne, Weston-Super-Mare, Skegness and Great Yarmouth staged contests, but the main focus was always the Lancashire and North Wales coast: Rhyl, New Brighton, Blackpool, Fleetwood, Morecambe and not least, Southport. The contests were a new kind of entertainment for the holidaymaker as the country moved on from the greyness and austerity of the war years. Fun for all the family, the men would enjoy watching pretty girls, the women would enjoy picking their favourites (or commenting on the others) and the little girls would dream of being bathing beauties when they grew up. Bathing belles from the length and breadth of Britain flocked here in the 1950s and 1960s to enter the famous Miss New Brighton and Southport's English Rose competitions, each of them hoping to walk away with the prized sash and a host of modelling contracts to choose from. With the regulation stilettos, swim suits and ribbons the pageants were the highlight of the summer calendar for many young women and their eager mothers. And the contests were extremely popular with growing audiences of holidaymakers. Fifteen thousand people were reported to have watched the first Miss New Brighton Final in 1949. The weekly heats, with the girls parading around the local swimming pool, would be watched by crowds of four or five thousand in the early years and they would often be judged by famous entertainers. Early judges of Miss Great Britain included actress Glynis Johns, comedian Bob Monkhouse, singer Guy Mitchell and even Laurel and Hardy. Not to be outdone, our own kings of comedy duo, Morecambe and Wise can be seen (pictured left) in 1964 with Southport's 'English Rose' finalists. The sea bathing lake was a hugely popular success and an ideal place to hold beauty contests. In the earlier picture from 1952 we can the finalists lined up in all their finery at the pool-side. It must have been quite blustery as a number of the girls are hanging onto their hats.

Right: Girls Aloud eat your hearts out. What a bonny set of lasses in this Rosebud group. Older girls competed for the title of Rose Queen, but interest was just as keen to see which tot would get the sash as the Rosebud. The honour on this occasion has obviously gone to the little blonde, second right. Why is it that brunettes so often miss out? The parents of these children would have been pleased that they had scrubbed up so well. Even so, they congratulated the winner's mother through gritted teeth, muttering something about judges not knowing their rosebuds from their elbows. On many occasions, the Southport Rosebud contest took place at the fitting venue of the Floral Pavilion. The town's connection with a flowery world began on 27 August, 1924, when a 'Grand Floral Fete' was held. According to advertising posters this included 'horse leaping'. The mind boggles! The event flourished as Southport Flower Show in the 1930s and, after being suspended during the war, was relaunched in 1947 and has gone from strength to strength ever since to gain an international reputation.

© Southport Visitor/Trinity Mirror North West

© Southport Visitor/Trinity Mirror North West

Below left: There are lots of exhibits at Southport Flower Show, but obviously by far the most interesting to this little girl in 1951, is a Punch & Judy made up of flowers. She is both mystified and fascinated and I think she would like to climb inside this floral theatre, to get a peak at what's going on backstage. Born just after the Second World War, she was one of the generation of baby boomers and just loved the mixture of hilarity and mayhem created 'before her very eyes', as Arthur Askey used to say. In the 20th century red-and-white-striped puppet booths became iconic features on the beaches of many English seaside and summer holiday resorts. Such striped cloth is the most common covering today, however in this case it is predominantly red & white flowers. Originally intended for adults, the show evolved into primarily a children's entertainment in the late Victorian era. Ancient members of the show's cast ceased to be included when they came to be seen as inappropriate for young audiences. The term "pleased as Punch" is derived from Punch and Judy; specifically, Mr. Punch's characteristic sense of gleeful self-satisfaction. He even has his own catchphrases which have stood the test of time: for example, Punch, after dispatching his foes each in turn, still squeaks his famous catchphrase: "that's the way to do it!!" The Flower Show is held annually in late August on the 34 acre site in Victoria Park. It is the largest independent flower show in the UK and can attract up to 100,000 visitors over the four days of the event.

Above: A very wintery scene from arctic conditions in 1955. Ice floes have been washed up by the tide on the shore in Southport. This lady, dressed for the conditions, is looking somewhat perplexed as to how they might have got there, but she is not missing the photo opportunity by standing on top of one of the solid ice structures. In mid January of that year snow falls of 5ft had been experienced in the North West and this continued into February causing drifting in blizzard conditions.

Below: On 18 February, 1988, Prince Andrew, Duke of York and his wife, the former Sarah Ferguson delighted us with a visit. Here the Duchess made friends with many for the warm way in which she greeted locals and accepted posies presented to her. At this time everything seemed sweetness and light for the royal couple. They became parents later that year, with birth of daughter Beatrice on 8 August, 1988. Their second child Eugenie was born on 23 March, 1990. They had been married for less than two years, but everlasting happiness was not to be theirs. The marriage was soon in difficulty as Andrew and Sarah drifted apart in the early 1990s.

Oh I do love to be beside the seaside. Our great grandparents enjoyed the sand and the water just as much as we do. They did so wearing a great deal more than in the 21st century or even in most of the last one. It seems odd to modern sun worshippers, who strip off at the merest hint of a glint from that yellow orb in the sky, that people once put on jackets or long dresses in order to spend a day on the beach. Rolled up trouser legs or slightly lifted skirts were about the most daring things that old Uncle Albert or Great Aunt Minnie would chance. Those who came here for their annual holidays made sure that they got onto the beach and sat on a deckchair come rain or shine. For many, this was their only break in the year from the drudgery of factory work or time spent standing by looms in the mills. Consequently, they made for the seashore and claimed their piece of sand. Of course, in Southport, the size of the beach meant that there was room for everyone.

ENTERTAINMENT
LEISURE & PASTIMES

Left: If you want to get ahead, get a hat. It would seem that the ladies on show in this 1906 outing had all favoured the same milliner. There is a distinct uniformity to the majority of headgear on show. In their charge that day was a fine collection of youngsters who attended Sunday School at the Trinity Wesleyan Chapel, built in 1864 at a cost of £9,000. Not satisfied with encouraging attendance at its morning services, many churches established classes known as 'Sunday Schools' that provided specialist religious education for young parishioners. Robert Raikes, the 18th century Gloucester philanthropist and Anglican preacher, is usually thought to have been a pioneer in this field. He saw these schools as an opportunity to educate both the minds and the souls of the children from the working classes. By the end of the 19th century, when children were now attending ordinary schools and most were learning to be literate and numerate, the emphasis turned to Bible studies and lessons on church dogma. The children needed a day out in the countryside as a bit of light relief.

Above and left: Now, do not try this at home. The lion cubs from Zoodrome were getting a telling off for being naughty little pussy cats, but the girl doing the scolding needed to be careful. Those teeth and claws were sharp. The inclusive price of admission to the Zoodrome and Empire Theatre was just a tanner (2.5p), but that was still a bit pricey when the average daily wage for the working man was only about four shillings (20p). This site was part of the former Winter Gardens that opened on the sea front in 1874, but were never very commercially successful despite having a zoo, skating rink, theatre, opera house and aquarium within the complex. The Winter Gardens were demolished in 1933.

An excited group of children play on Formby sands in front of the Stella Maris Hotel. Although built in 1905 as a hotel, it was never used as such. During its fifty years in existence it had a number of uses, including a convalescent home for priests, a holiday home for catholic children, a café, and a radar station during the Second World War. After the war the building became derelict and was eventually demolished in 1954.

Sitting on the sands, with the marram grass and dunes as a backdrop, provided endless days of rest and relaxation for hundreds of trippers and holidaymakers every day of the week throughout the summer in the heyday of holidays at home. It was not until the 1960s that we started to abandon our traditional beaches and look for warmer climes that had a more reliable source of constant sunshine. In those days, before packages and tours abroad, we were happy with the lot we had. Games of cricket that went on all day, granddad snoozing in a deckchair with a hankie on his head and mum being buried in the sand were perfectly normal family pastimes that kept us all entertained.

Throw in the occasional donkey ride, an ice cream cornet doused in raspberry and a Punch and Judy show and our ecstasy knew no bounds. Britain's first lifeboat station was here by 1776. The last launch took place in 1916, when the Lifeboat station was finally closed. It was used as a cafe on the beach from 1918 until its demolition in 1965. The ruins of a later station, built on the original site can still be seen on the beach today. Until 1940, when it was demolished, visitors to Formby Sands could look at the lighthouse that had occupied this stretch of coast since 1719. It had only been used briefly as a lighthouse, serving most of its time as a simple landmark to help sailors

navigate the Mersey passage. It was for a similar reason that it was taken down, being too useful to German planes intent on attacking Liverpool during the Blitz. Formby Point has one of the longest and largest stretches of dunes in England. Backed by the pine forests where animal life abounds, it is one of the most unspoiled parts of the English coastline.

Left: Young ladies of a certain class were encouraged to take polite exercise as part of their education. It is thought that this setting was Beaconholm Girls' College, even though the original image is marked 'Lendal'. What is not in dispute is that tennis on the lawn was seen as an acceptable pastime for daughters of the gentry. In fact, such a word was seldom used when referring to delicate souls like these. They were there to study etiquette as much as any academic subject and the ability to organise servants in the household was as important as any proficiency in scientific matters. The world that they knew was one where nannies and governesses had their parts to play. There were maids galore, both upstairs and downstairs. People spoke of being from 'good stock' and were graded as suitors accordingly. It was a style of living that persisted for the middle and upper classes until the time of the First World War, when the world order changed for evermore.

Right: Plans were made in 1874 to create the Botanic Gardens at Churchtown, on the site of the former Strawberry Gardens, they were opened the following year by Reverend Charles Hesketh, one of an important family of local landowners. Other buildings, including refreshment rooms and a museum, were added in 1876. The grand greenhouse was a fine centrepiece to the gardens and housed many exotic plants. The grounds include a lovely lake that was part of the Otter Pool, a stream that flowed through Meols Hall and on to the sea. The gardens deteriorated into a sorry state during the interwar years and lay derelict by 1932. Happily, the Hesketh family came to the rescue and, thanks to the generosity of Roger Fleetwood Hesketh, a future MP and High Sheriff of Lancashire, the town was able to purchase the grounds and restore them to former glories in 1937 as a memorial to the late King George V. In 2011, Sefton Council controversially decided to cut back on the cost of supporting the Botanic Gardens, closing its museum and reducing the horticultural activities.

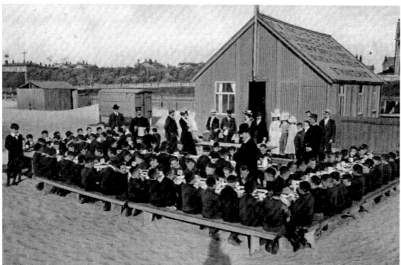

Left: The Poor Boys' Camp was part of the Victorian determination to provide help for the less fortunate and, at the same time, offer them guidance for the future. Land on the seaward side of the Esplanade and the old Cheshire Lines Railway was put to use from about 1870 onwards as a summer camp. Boys from impoverished circumstances in the Manchester area were brought here and offered a mixture of instruction and recreation that would improve them physically, mentally and morally. The timing of the founding of the camp matched the introduction of the 1870 Elementary Education Act that introduced schooling for all children aged between five and twelve. This was seen as an extension of the work of the Poor Law Unions. This Southport camp, pictured during the first decade of the last century,

came under threat in 1911 when the landlord, Charles Weld-Blundell, proposed that a housing development be built on the site. Happily, he was unsuccessful and the camp, with its collection of huts and tents, continued in existence for some years longer. Today, the site is managed as a nature reserve.

Above and below: The images on this page are a snapshot of children in a Day Nursery for Excursionists on Southport beach. Not the orthodox type of nursery that allows parents to go out to work, but a place where overworked parents could leave their children, for a few hours, whilst they enjoy themselves on holiday. On the shore, near the the pier at

Southport, a large portion of the beach was set aside for the day nursery which was devoted almost exclusively to the excursionists. For the princely sum of sixpence, a child or baby could be left all day at the nursery managed by a commitee of ladies under the presidency of the mayoress of Southport. It was a bit like handing your coat in at the theatre, you received a ticket, whilst a similar ticket was attached to the child. On your return you handed in your ticket and your child was handed over. How times have changed. Although there are still organised children's clubs at hotels in holiday resorts, it's hard to imagine handing the kids over to a stranger on the shore.

Below inset: What marvellous fun was to be had and what a wide and wonderful range of activities were provided for our forebears a century ago. We may regard the dodgems, carousels, roundabouts, coconut shies and helter skelter as run of the mill attractions, but they were once something of a novelty. Seeing so much in one place was a treat seldom experienced before. The water chute that opened in 1903 at the southern end of Marine Lake was particularly popular. The excited squeals of the girls and the merry laughter of the boys let you know that everyone was having a whale of a time. Behind the chute, the Flying Machine was doing good business. It opened in c1906 and the gondolas spinning around on the frame owed something in their design to the early Zeppelin airship. This was the era when powered flight was achieved by the Wright brothers at Kitty Hawk and interest in this field developed apace. The machine was designed by Hiram Maxim. The inventor was born in America in 1840 and is best remembered across the globe for the machine gun he developed. A born tinkerer with things, he was involved in attempts to produce such varied items as the first lightbulb and aeroplane, though failed to lead the way in either field. He was more successful in his military exploits. He emigrated to Britain in 1881 and became a naturalised citizen in 1899. By then he had perfected the killing machine that would become the standard machine gun used by the British Army for many years. The fairground gradually moved away from the lake during the 1910s and was remodelled as Pleasureland in 1922.

Above: The aerial shot of the fairground in the 1950s conjures up images of delightful times spent after the war when people could rest easy and enjoy themselves without an anxious look up at the skies in case a German fighter of bomber was on the prowl. You can almost smell the aroma of candy floss and toffee apples. Cars were parked up on the sands and people flocked from the beach to the dodgems and back again. Pop music blared out as the waltzers spun from side to side. There was a variety, ranging from Guy Mitchell's 'She wears red feathers' to Elvis Presley's 'Hound Dog', being played through the tannoys. It was great to be young and free and we made the most of it.

Local builder, Thomas Stanley carried out the construction of Southport Town Hall in 10 months, from a design by architect Thomas Withnell in 1852/53. Essentially classical, the building, which can be seen on the left in these two images, is made up of a mixture of architectural styles, and in the pediment above the 17ft high porch, a design was carved which pictures three figures representing Justice, Truth and Mercy. Next to this is the Cambridge Arcade separating the Town Hall from the other Municipal Buildings, which now include Southport Arts Centre, the Atkinson Art Gallery and the library. The most prominent building in these two early images is The Cambridge Hall, which today is called The Arts Centre. It was designed by Maxwell & Tuke and was opened by Richard Asherton Cross, Secretary of State, on 6 October, 1874. Above the skyline, at either end of the building, we have a high clock tower and a small turret. The Atkinson Art Gallery was designed by Waddington and Sons, of Burnley, and completed in 1878. To the right hand side of the picture below is the West Lancashire Bank however, this is now an extension of the library. Fronting the Municipal Buildings are the Municipal Gardens.

Clearly visible in the bottom picture is the monument to Queen Victoria, which can be seen in it's original site before being moved to Nevill Street in 1912. A feature of the gardens at the time was the bandstand with its columns, balustrades and fountains. Unbelievably, the gardens were dismantled in 1969 and it would be 30 years before they were fully remodelled using some of the detail from Thomas Mawson's original scheme. The gardens are now known as Princess Diana Gardens following the death of the ever-popular Princess.

Walter Connard established the jewellers firm of Connard & Son in 1883. In 1912 he built the Palladium Picture Palace cinema of which he was the managing director until 1922. In 1913 through talks with the local council its was agreed that he could develop the land in front of the cinema into St George's Gardens on the condition they a sculpture designed and financed by him was sitied within the park. The Palladium was burnt down on the 26 March, 1929, and only the facade remained. It was rebuilt by Gaumont-British and re-opened as the New Palladium in October, 1930, but on an enlarged site as can be seen if you compare these photographs. It was situated in fashionable Lord Street and had formerly been a noted cine-variety theatre. There were approx 700 seats in the balcony and 1,500 in the stalls. The 'New' was dropped from the re-opening name of New Palladium and, in 1950, it was renamed Gaumont. In 1962 it became Odeon. Around this time the Beatles were playing several live nightly concerts at the Gaumont

which had a small stage suitable for performances once the screen was removed. Rank closed the Odeon on 28 November, 1979. After a long decline the supermarket chain Sainsbury's made an offer for the site, and despite its Listed building status permission was granted to demolish the Odeon in the summer of 1980.

Two images of the Palace Cinema, Southport, over 40 years apart. The earliest of the two pictures was taken around the time of the opening in 1911. The Palace was one of several cinemas in the town which would be designed by local architect George E. Tonge. The exterior of the building was a splendid example of Edwardian Baroque style. The date we know to be fairly accurate as the film, 'Janet's Flirtation' was released in 1911 and starred teenage actress Chrissie White. An actress from the early days of the British cinema, she was born in 1895 and lived until the age of 94. In 1929 the Palace closed for a major re-construction and the cafe became the balcony foyer. It re-opened as the Palace Cinema in March 1930.

The second image (below) shows the Palace in 1953, promoting a giant panoramic screen. It became the first independently operated cinema in the UK to screen "Around the World in Eighty Days", which ran for 11 weeks in 1958. It came under the control of the Essoldo chain from March 1971 and was re-named Essoldo, but they were soon taken over by Classic Cinemas chain and it was re-named Classic Cinema in 1972. A further change in the 80s led to a take-over by the Cannon Group. The cinema was closed in January 2003.

Above: The Palace Hotel opened for business in 1866 when Birkdale was a separate borough in its own right. It was built at a cost of £60,000 on a 20 ace site at the end of Weld Road, fronting the sea, though its main entrance area looks away from the coast. Some have suggested that the builders had architect William Mangnall's plans the wrong way round and that this caused him to commit suicide by jumping to his death from the hotel roof. Despite attempting to prove that the hotel was thus both blighted and haunted, there appears to be little truth in either suggestion and Mangnall actually died of TB. From 1884, the hotel had a rail link to the outside world and, in 1919, was connected to the skies by an aviation service from a small airfield close by that flew in patrons from Blackpool. The connection with things aeronautical was advanced during World War II. The hotel was taken over by the Americans in 1942 and used by their Red Cross as a rest home for recuperating members of the US 8th Army Air Force who had been on bombing raids across Europe. It was run by volunteers who organised dances, socials and sporting activities for those billeted there. After the war, things went back to normal and the hotel was occasionally used as a film set. Clark Gable and Frank Sinatra are said to have stayed there. The hotel closed in 1967 and was demolished in 1969, with the exception of its coach house that is now the Fishermen's Rest public house.

Above right: The classical stone, moulded balustrades and orb lamps on top of short pillars are a feature of a good stretch of the eastern side of Lord Street in the town centre. This section,

leading to Cambridge Arcade and near the front of the Arts Centre, the former Cambridge Hall, is part of the Municipal Gardens. The Town Gardens Café, a self-styled 'continental establishment,' could be found here. This was a pleasant spot in which to enjoy an expresso. It was rehoused in a pavilion in 1999, not too far from where the similarly modern Tourist Information Centre can now be seen further along on the corner of Eastbank Street. Some of the designs for the gardens created by Thomas Mawson in the early 1900s are still with us, but the

magnificent bandstand, admired by so many, was lost when it was dismantled in 1969, despite a furore of protests. The remodelled landscaped area was then known as the Civic Gardens, but became the Princess Diana Gardens after her death in 1997.

Above: Our town has only a short span in terms of being an entity in its own right. As with many other coastal towns, its development was aided by the coming of the railways and the new interest in sea bathing as both a recreation and a curative in the early 19th century. The north of England, in particular, spawned new marine towns and industrial cities in abundance. Until then, the west Lancashire coast had been bypassed for human settlement and interests, with small exceptions at North Meols, Churchtown and South Hawes. When the Bold and Hesketh families helped lay out the streets, they legislated for a pattern that was largely made up of detached houses or semis. Little in the way of terraced homes was ever built here. This aided the establishment of Southport's reputation as a more genteel resort than any of its neighbours. This scene from the middle of the last century illustrates the popularity the sands and surrounds had acquired as a residential holiday destination as well as one for the day trippers. The pier has survived

collisions, fires and storms over the last 150 years, but nearly came to grief in 1990 when Sefton Council came within one vote of closing it.

Right: We can only stand and admire the craft of the sand artist as he creates marvellous tableaux from the material with which we struggle to form a simple, small castle on the beach. On 4 July, 1936, this chap was working away on various animal and human figures. His appeal for money to help him out is not surprising as these were the days when the unemployed marched from Jarrow and millions of others found themselves in dire straits during the period known as the Great Depression. Sand artists often included war victims who had lost limbs and struggled to survive in those difficult times before the welfare state came into being. Too proud to ask, they showed the world that they had something more than a begging bowl to offer.

Pleasureland was opened in King's Gardens, in 1912, initially with a Helter Skelter lighthouse and figure eight rollercoaster as the main attractions for the public. A similar helter skelter stood at the entrance to the Please Beach in Blackpool from 1905. In the early years, the park was grew at a rapid rate and the addition of a water chute and a Hiram Maxim Flying Machine meant the park had outgrown its site and in 1924, the rides and attractions were re-located to a new beachfront site. In 1928 one of the best known of all modern fairground rides was introduced into Britain by Messrs Lusse Brothers. The Dodgem had been in existence for a number of years abroad, but their popularity in Britain was soon established as amusement park attractions. Although the idea is to "dodge" other cars, the opportunity to drive around at random "bumping" into other cars, was much more fun and this led to the name 'bumper cars'. By the mid to late 1930s, Dodgems were the most popular fairground ride.

In 1947 the American influence can be seen on the left-hand drive petrol-powered two-seaters. Racing around the oval speedway track at the Peter Pan Playgound gender stereotypes were being reinforced when Don Hodgkiss took the wheel with Velma Blackburn as a happy passenger. All Don and Velma wanted to do was to have fun. They deserved to enjoy every minute of their time on the dodgems, big dipper, speedway cars, caterpillar and swing boats. The vast majority of their childhood had been spent worrying about their dads serving in the forces and how their mums were managing to juggle the meagre rations on which they had to feed and clothe their families. Now all that was behind them and the bluebirds had returned over the white cliffs once more. Britain had won its war and it was only right that its children should enjoy the benefits of peacetime.

Right: Many local readers from the Ainsdale and Formby area will recognise this building, but probably not as it is seen here as the Plaza Cinema. The Plaza, on Liverpool Road, encorporated a ballroom and cinema from the 1930s up until it closed in 1957. It may be more recognisable as the Moulin Rouge, where you could wine, dine and dance. It was also the place for regular live music and on a Wednesday evening, in May 1967, it was the venue for a Pink Floyd psychedelic pop gig. They also appeared on 20 May at the Floral Hall in Southport. By the mid-70s it had changed to Tiffany's nightclub and in the 80s became Ainsdale Country Club and 5th Avenue Bar, before being demolished in 1987. Today, the Toby Carvery stands on the site next to the Shell Service Station.

Below: This picture brings together young and old, as children of all ages reflect on the significance of the War Memorial and gardens. Built in 1923, the 20m-high central obelisk is flanked on either side by two pavilions of Roman Doric colonnades. The boys can be seen staring at their reflection in one of the two pools in the adjacent gardens on either side. The cost of around £30,000 was met by subscriptions from the public after an appeal was launched in 1919. Most thought provoking are the names of the dead from the Second World War and subsequent conflicts, listed at either end of the two pavilions. These were added to the Colonnades in 1992.

Above: On 7 November, 1953, the local repertory company was staging a season of plays at the Scala Theatre that included Terence Rattigan's 'The Deep Blue Sea'. This had only premiered in the West end of London the previous year and was about to be produced on Broadway this same week. The plot involves a woman who has left her husband for a semi alcoholic and then attempts to commit suicide. Needless to say, the storyline is not supposed to be a bundle of laughs. The Scala was formerly a concert hall and part of the old Winter Gardens that were, in the main, demolished in the early 1930s. It closed in the 1960s.

Left and above: After the Opera House burned down in 1929, the site was cleared and George E. Tonge, a Southport based architect, prepared plans for a new theatre which opened on 19 December, 1932. It was, and remains, a glorious exercise in Art Deco style, inside and out. A massive building in red brick with stone dressings, the stage was particularly large, and was designed to accommodate touring drama, musicals, opera and ballet. At the time, the theatre was advertised as the most beautiful in Europe. Situated on the main Southport thoroughfare of Lord Street, the Garrick initially operated as a live venue only. Local and international variety artists appeared to packed houses. Older readers may remember such names as Frank Randall, Lita Rosa, Dickie Valentine and even a one-off appearance by Laurel and Hardy in 1952. In 1957, it was sold to the Essoldo Cinemas group but continued to present live shows in addition to films after this time. As audiences melted away, cinema owners sought new uses for the huge capacity buildings. Some cinema theatres became bingo halls as this form of entertainment became popular. Inevitably, this happened at the Garrick and it closed in November 1963 and was converted into a Lucky 7 bingo club, later Top Rank and Mecca.

Above and right: Ballroom dancing has made a comeback in recent years, largely due to BBC TV coverage of its celebrity 'Strictly Come Dancing' competition. At one time everybody at least knew how to waltz, quickstep and foxtrot. For the slightly more daring we could also manage a passable cha-cha-cha and rumba, though the samba was possibly a bit too much for most of us to handle. Learning the basic turn, glide and chassis was essential in the courting game. No lad with two left feet was ever going to get the pretty girl to take his arm. Similarly, any lass who could not fishtail her way along the floor during the quickstep was destined for wallflower status. Dancing was also a necessary social skill. Heaven help the young executive who trod on the toes of the boss's wife at the annual dinner dance! The big band sound was in evidence at the Floral Hall in the picture above with a vast, slow-moving circle of waltzing and foxtrotting dancers, where god forbid any couple who attempted to jive. In 1877 the gardens in front of the municipal buildings were redesigned to include a fountain and bandstand and in the picture on the right members of the crowd dance along at an open air concert.

Right: The handsome bandstand in the Municipal Gardens was just the place to while away a comfortable hour in the early years of the last century. Local ensembles, brass bands and small orchestras used this platform for a mixture of pleasure, performance and practice. The audience simply enjoyed the entertainment, especially when the sun shone. The bandstand underwent a number of changes either side of the 1914-18 War, but never altered in its level of popularity. It was lost to the town in 1969 when it was demolished and the area landscaped. However, a link with the past was re-established when a new Victorian-style, iron replacement was erected in the 1980s, close to the Lord Street corner with Market Street.

An orderly queue gathers outside the Regal Cinema, on the corner of Wellington Street, waiting to gain entrance to see the critically acclaimed Battle of Britain film 'Angels One Five'. The picture was taken in 1952 and it would appear the audience are due for a special treat in the shape of a personal appearance from English motion picture, stage and television actress, Veronica Hurst, who starred in the film alongside Jack Hawkins and John Gregson. The Regal opened in December 1938 and was designed by architect William R.

Glen. It had a capacity of over 1,600 seats, despite being built on a relatively small plot of land. The cinema was renamed the ABC in 1962, when the corner facade was modernised, as can be seen in the second photograph from 18 February, 1963. The cinema survived through the Fifties and Sixties, presenting performances three times daily, often showing films in the summer season ahead of national release. Unfortunately, cinema audiences started to decline and this eventually led to the closure of the cinema in 1984. Demolition took place in the summer of 1987 and a block of retirement flats was built on the site.

Below: This dapper gentleman made a living out of playing upper class twits and cads. Often seen sporting a cigarette holder below a raffish moustache, his gap toothed smile adorned many a cinema poster in the middle years of the last century. Here riding Gertrude the donkey in a publicity shoot during the summer of 1953, Terry-Thomas attracted an audience of modest proportions. Born Thomas Terry Hoar Stevens in 1911, he worked initially as a clerk. He dabbled in show business in the 1930s before establishing a cabaret act during the war. However, it was during the 1950s that he was to make a breakthrough into television and films as an upper class rascal. One of his catchphrases, 'You're an absolute shower' was created in a Boulting Brothers' comedy, the 1956 movie 'Private's Progress'. His distinctive voice was mimicked by Ivan Owen for the puppet Basil Brush. During the 1960s he was in constant demand, starring in such movie box office hits as 'It's a Mad, Mad, Mad, Mad World', 'Those Magnificent Men in Their Flying Machines' and 'Monte Carlo or Bust'. He retired in the late 1970s suffering from Parkinson's disease and died in 1990.

Above: This could be something from one of Enid Blyton's stories. Perhaps it is 'The Famous Five Explore the Botanic Gardens'. The children look to be off on an adventure. Imagine the fuss there would be nowadays that kiddies could take to the water unaccompanied by an adult. Yet, when you were a youngster, surely you needed some time to yourself in the company of a peer group without grown-ups to fuss all over you? Located in the pretty district of Churchtown, this parkland is sometimes called Southport's 'jewel in the crown'. The lake winds its way the length of gardens that offer an abundance of floral displays to gladden even the toughest heart. The Botanic gardens opened in 1874 and have been a joy ever since.

Below: London Square is the centre of the retail and commercial world of the town. Situated on Lord Street, where London Street heads away to the right and Nevill Street to the left, the War Memorial and its pair of pavilions and colonnades now dominate the scene. In Edwardian times, as we can observe here, horse drawn vehicles happily co-

existed alongside the then very modern style of public transport that was the tram. Passengers on the top deck enjoyed the journey on summer days, but it was a distinctly draughty and uncomfortable experience when the sea breezes and Lancashire rain had an impact. The handsome building in the centre of the picture is the only one actually on the square to date from the 19th century, despite the classical look of some others here. The National Westminster Bank, now NatWest, was designed by William and Segar Owen from Warrington. Built in the Renaissance style, it is complemented by the Post Office building to its left that also has a Victorian heritage.

Above: The covered-top trams and the presence of the War Memorial in London Square tell us that this image was captured in c1924. Horse drawn trams were established by private companies in the 19th century, with Southport Tramways being among the pioneers in this form of public transport. It was formed in 1871 and, by 1873, had established a route between Churchtown and Birkdale Station. The Corporation bought the Southport part of the operation in 1899, converting it for use by electric traction the following year. This became part of the British Electric Traction Company's franchise as more routes were electrified from 1901 onwards. The Corporation did not take over full control of the area's tramways until the end of the 1914-18 War. The last tram ran in 1935, by which time buses were seen as a more reliable and profitable mode of public transport.

Right: Hold very tight, please. It will soon be time for the off. Americans like to take the grand tour of Europe. We in Lancashire are quite happy with one on an open topped tram along the Promenade, Esplanade, Marine Drive and, perhaps, a bit of Lord Street. Well, at least we were the best part of a century ago, but it was going to be a day for wrapping up as best you could against the elements. The British are a hardy race. Can you imagine our cousins from across the big pond indulging in such a trip along the sea front, coats buttoned up and hats pulled down tight? It would be enough to make their hot dogs curl and French fries freeze.

Above: A characterful scene from Lord Street, possibly around 1920. The tram stands motionless as a group of predominately female passenger get on board. The style of clothes looks to be more of a practical nature and this could be as a result of necessity during the First World War. Clothes became more practical and less restrictive and were now cut so that movement was not hampered. The tram would have been run by Southport Corporation until closure on 31 December, 1934.

Below: The Lancashire and Yorkshire Railway Company was founded in 1847. At its peak, it owned 1,650 locomotives and was the country's most densely packed railway, in terms of locos per mile of track. The station at Chapel Street opened in 1851 as a replacement for the former terminus of the Southport and Crosby Railway in Eastbank Street. It became the terminus for all trains from Wigan in 1857 when passenger services were transferred from the station at London Street. One time Chapel Street Station had eleven passenger platforms and two designated for excursion use. Although much changed in appearance today, especially after remodelling in the early 1970s and again more recently, it still functions here under the simple name of Southport Railway Station.

Above: The handsome motorcade held a mixture of dignitaries, army officers and nurses. They had assembled in readiness for the opening of the Voluntary Aid Detachment (VAD) Hospital. Having left the cars behind, the local gentry strolled along the drive, flanked by a guard of honour formed by a line of nurses. High ranking officers, dressed in their best uniforms, joined them as they listened to the address given by the Mayor. The VAD was founded in 1909 by the Red Cross and the Order of St John to provide field nursing services, but mainly based in hospitals. Southport's hospital and its nurses supported the more formally trained nurses who were overstretched by the demands placed upon them in World War I. Wounded soldiers did not worry too much about who was at their bedside. They were grateful to get a helping hand and see a smiling face. Some 9,000 women and girls had enrolled in the VAD by the end of 1914. Authors Vera Brittain and Agatha Christie both served in this organisation and variously drew on their experiences in their later writings.

Bottom left: As the shore is such a mighty length, buses used to deliver passengers to various points there in order to save a bit of legwork for those of a more sedentary nature. After the last war, DUKW (colloquially called 'duck') amphibious vehicles were also used to ferry people along the sands to Ainsdale. These six-wheel-drive trucks had been used by the American military in landings in Italy and Normandy during the war and became very popular in peacetime giving kiddies rides through the shallows. They were also used by lifeguards as a sea rescue vehicle for many years.

Below: Standing at the lay-by, outside where the Tourist Information Centre can be found today, the open-top bus had just completed a sightseeing tour of the sea front and Lord Street. Resting on Eastbank Street on 22 July, 1984, the Weyman bodied Leyland Titan was enjoying a well earned break. The Old Bank, now a wine bar, can just be seen to the right. The main part of the picture is dominated by the Scarisbrick Hotel. It was erected in 1889 on the site of the Scarisbrick Arms Hotel that had stood here for 60 years. Built by Thomas Mawdsley, it was known at first as the Hesketh Arms, after a former Lord of the Manor. The new hotel could accommodate 120 guests and boasted the finest safety devices in rendering it almost fireproof, or so it claimed. The Scarisbrick also had a state of the art passenger lift. The name had been changed in honour of Charles Scarisbrick, an important member of the county set. The hotel was well known in the hare coursing world and an early proprietor, E W Stocker, was a noted owner of a dog that won the prestigious Waterloo Cup.

Below and right: There is nothing on our railways today that can compare with the steam locomotives of yesteryear. Why else do we still flock to take a trip on the Ribble Steam Railway, the East Lancashire Railway or even go across the border and hop aboard a carriage belonging to the Keighley and Worth Valley Railway? That evocative hiss of steam takes those of us with balding pates and greying locks back to our youth. We hung over bridges as the mighty machines thundered by beneath our feet and packed up sandwiches and bottles of Tizer to get us through a day at Chapel Street station. Having bought a platform ticket, we spent ages carefully recording locomotive numbers and wheel arrangements in well thumbed exercise books. If we look in the loft at home, we might even find those still intact, inside an old knapsack awaiting rediscovery. The loco pulling the carriages that was headed away from the signal box was No 50781. It was withdrawn from service in February 1960. The accompanying photograph demonstrates just how important a station Chapel Street has been over the years, serving a large number of lines to platforms that numbered in double figures in its heyday.

Right: Formby Station is now on the Southport branch of Merseyrail's Northern line. It dates back to 1848 when the original station was built by the Liverpool, Southport and Crosby Railway Company. It became part of the Lancashire and Yorkshire Railway in 1904 and, after one more change, emerged in 1923 as part of the LMS. This special six car diesel multiple unit (DMU) train is thought to have been chartered by the Orange Lodge in Liverpool for an excursion to Southport and is seen here on the return journey in the late 1970s. Large fleets of DMUs were built by British Railways in the late 1950s and 1960s, though the first ones had appeared in some parts of the country before the last war.

AT WORK

Below: You could imagine George Formby singing a ditty about the business that used these vans to get the laundry collected, dealt with and back to its customers as quickly and as cleanly as possible. Established in 1875, the Southport Steam Laundry was taken over by a married couple named Benson in 1883. They invested in patent ironing machines, several washing machines that included an American hydraulic model and a Troy collar and cuff ironer that provided a truly professional finish. The largest ironer catered for tablecloths up to nearly eight feet in width, making some people wonder at the size of tables in certain households. There was a special room for curtain framing and the treatment of woollen goods such as blankets and flannel items. The cleaning of dresses and shirts was advertised as 'our speciality'.

Above: A picture from 1920 of workers shovelling coal on to a coal conveyor at Formby power station. Coal was the main fuel source used in power stations at this time and was brought by rail and passed from the wagons into the building via the chute. This power station was built to provide electricity to supply the Liverpool to Southport railway line. Electrification began in 1904 to provide faster and more efficient services on this busy line and it took 12 months to electrify the 23 miles of double track from Liverpool to Crossens. The power station closed in 1946 but the building was later used by Metal Closures Rosslite Ltd and then as a business centre, before becoming derelict

Above: Could one of these boys at Holmwood School on Barkfield Lane, have become the next Thomas Chippendale? It is hardly likely they were carving out the next Queen Anne-style Cabriole leg, but the work was enjoyable and much more preferable to cooking and sewing with the girls. At the time schools, unlike today, encouraged different skills for the two sexes. The site of the school became a housing development in the 1990s.

Silcock Leisure
All the Fun of the Fair...and More

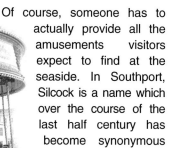

Silcock's famous Golden Gallopers carousel in Southport features three cockerels and 33 horses. But what are the names of those fabulous beasts? That's a mystery, the answer to which is known to but a special few.

The Golden Gallopers ride represents the very epitome of the fairground, which along with rides, sun, sand and ice-cream are part of the iconic image of the seaside.

Seaside holidays are embedded in all our minds. Every child wants to go to the seaside. And every adult remembers the seaside of their own childhood, back when the days were always long, the sun was always warm, the sea was even saltier and the donkeys twice as large. But the seaside funfairs. Ah the seaside funfairs of yesteryear. The rides, the coconut shy, dodgems, candy-floss, bright lights and even brighter music.

Was there ever a child born who did not yearn to visit the funfair? Or any adult whose heart doesn't still beat a little faster to hear that magic word?

Of course, someone has to actually provide all the amusements visitors expect to find at the seaside. In Southport, Silcock is a name which over the course of the last half century has become synonymous with entertainment.

Silcock Leisure is a fifth generation family business, with over a century of experience in the amusement business – from Silcocks' long-ago Travelling Fairs of Warrington, and four decades based at Southport's Pleasureland, to today's modern Family Amusement Centres and restaurants in both Southport and Blackpool.

Edward Silcock senior founded Silcock's Travelling Fairs, which fully lived up to the name by travelling all over the north of England entertaining the public. All four sons of Edward Silcock (Lawrence, Edward, Herbert and Arthur) went into the same business as their father.

Above: The Golden Gallopers, Silcock's flagship ride. *Below:* The Silcock's 'Flyer' swingboat in the 1880s.

In the late 1950s Edward senior's grandson, Herbert Silcock, and his wife Jane, established themselves with rides at Southport's Pleasureland. The couple first met in 1943 when the fair Herbert was working on visited Aspull, near Wigan, where Jane lived. They spent the day together, but parted later that night thinking they would never see each other again. A year later the couple's paths crossed a second time when they both attended a dance at the Wigan Empress.

Celebrating 60 years of marriage in 2009, Jane, by then 83, said: "I was singing at the Empress when Herbert came up to me. I was so surprised. We danced the last waltz together and then we arranged to meet up for our first date." Herbert, 82, added: "When I saw Jane singing I thought 'I know that girl' and I went over to speak to her. For our first date I took her for a walk down Wigan Lane!"

The couple were engaged soon after, with Jane helping out at Herbert's family fairs every weekend.

On February 14, 1949, Herbert and Jane were married at a small ceremony held at Warrington Parish Church. After honeymooning in Dublin, the Silcocks got back to work building what would become their entertainment empire, with both Herbert and Jane working together every day, travelling with the fair.

They moved to Southport in 1959 and since then the pair, together with their family, have built a vast business portfolio.

The Silcock story however, all started in the 1880s with Edward Silcock's 'Flyer' and a coconut shy.

*Above: Herbert Silcock aged 21 minding his stall. **Below:** Just Married, Herbert and Jane Silcock pictured on their wedding day in 1949.*

Edward's four sons began travelling just before the First World War, their rides soon became popular attractions at fairs across the North West. The Silcock's family association with Southport started when they rented a piece of land from the Hesketh Family to operate their first travelling fair in Churchtown, Southport. They then moved to Blowick and then on to their current site in Stamford Road in Birkdale after the war along with Matt Morans' famous boxing booth.

However, the family really made a name for itself at the Warrington Potato Market and through operating a number of 'Holiday at Home' fairs during the Second World War, at which

Above: The Silcock brothers at work assembling their rides at the annual 'Warrington Walking Day' festival in the 1930s. Below: The Silcock General Gordon Gaviolli Organ which is still in the ownership of the family.

Victoria Park, Warrington. This was largely due to the association with the previous Holiday at Home fairs held in the park. In 1949 the World's Fair correspondent, the Burnley Cyclist, reports that: 'At Victoria Park, Warrington, Silcock Bros had a grand array of amusements for the 'Walking Day' festival. On Friday, the main day, business was good. The lovely orchestrations were like new. The Swirl organ having a picture of a circus parade over the top. The Dodgem has a big organ at the side which was known as the General Gordon (bottom, facing page), is a treat and the Noah's Ark with Arthur in command is a popular machine each time it visits.'

This page: *Various Silcock rides in Pleasureland.*

evening rides and attraction operated under blackout covers. They also ran a fair at Daisy Nook, Failsworth, Greater Manchester, a scene which was memorably captured by L S Lowry in his famous painting Good Friday Daisy Nook.

By the early 1940s Silcock was already a well-established name. During the Second World War 'Big Ted', Lawrence, Herbert and Arthur, the original Silcock brothers, put on their 'Holidays at Home Fairs' at Warrington's Victoria Park. Holidays at Home was a nationwide wartime initiative designed to allow folk to have an annual holiday even though the war meant they could not travel to the usual holiday resorts.

After 1945 and war's end the annual 'Walking Day Fair' was held in Catholic Fields and

Silcocks plan new amusement centre

A NEW amusement centre is due to open in Southport at Easter following the purchase of the empty, four-storey Woosey's Star Cafe and Restaurant by showman Mr. Herbert Silcock and his family.

Mr. Silcock, Chairman of the Southport Section of B.A.C.T.A. and one of the major concessionaires on the resort's Pleasureland amusement park, told the "World's Fair" that he had been negotiating for the premises on the corner of Coronation Walk and West Street near the promenade for the past two years.

All his immediate family are partners in the new venture, comprising Mrs. Jane Silcock and their daughter Pauline and two sons, Herbert, Jnr., and Mark.

Woosey's Star Cafe, once one of Southport's best-known catering establishments for holidaymakers and day outing parties, as well as for local functions, closed three years ago when brothers Bill and Fred Woosey retired. The business was started about 70 years ago.

The cafe has four floors. The ground floor, measuring about 50ft. x 40ft., will be varied amusements. The three shops on the corner and running along West Street are to be knocked into an ice-cream and fancy goods shop,

with access from the street and also from the arcade itself.

Mr. Silcock said it was planned to have the ground floor conversion completed in time for Easter at the end of March. The second floor will be devoted to table games, such as pool and air hockey.

The final phase of the conversion will be flats, probably for staff, on the third and fourth floors.

Mr. Silcock said he was hoping a start would be made very soon on the premises.

● Seen at the recent Southport B.A.C.T.A. dinner are Herbert Silcock and his family who will all be involved in the new development in the Woosey's Café premises. Left to right: Herbert, Jnr., Jane and her husband Herbert, Pauline and Mark.

In peacetime the fair became larger and by 1952 had doubled in size and included rides presented by the Silcock Brothers, J.J. Butterworth, J. Ryan. E. Morley, W. Shaw and F. Thompson among others. Other Walking Days such as Padgate and Stockton Heath, although not as a large as Warrington, were always well attended over the years. The run of fairs that made up the Walking Day Fairs traditionally started with Rainforth, and became known as the 'tea party' run in Lancashire.

In 1955 the Burnley Cyclist also reported an exciting incident at Padgate Walking Day fair, an event which had featured Silcock attractions since 1915: 'I heard of a gallant action by the showmen during their visit to Padgate. Nearby an aeroplane came down in a crash-landing. The showmen rushed to the spot and managed to get the airman clear. They were Fred

Brewer, J. Cook, J. Smith, Henshaw Bros, young Ted Silcock, and one or two others'.

Having established themselves in Southport in the 1950s, Herbert Silcock and his wife Jane continued to expand their business during the heyday of the seaside amusement park.

In the early 1980s the Silcocks opened their first family amusement centre in Coronation Walk, Southport, and with their three children, Herbert, Pauline and Mark, formed the Silcock Leisure Group.

Today, the Silcock Leisure Group encompasses, Funland and the Pier Fish & Chip restaurant, at the gateway to Southport Pier and is the town's largest such enterprise; Silcock's Leisure Casino, Funtime Amusements, Jackpot Amusements and Caesar's Amusements are all in Southport's Nevill Street along with Southport's oldest fish and chip restaurant, The Embassy, and the brand new 'Flavours' ice cream and coffee bar, whilst Carousel Amusements and the Fun Palace can be found on the famous Golden Mile in Blackpool.

But pride of place, however, must go to Silcock's Golden Gallopers Carousel, featuring those three cockerels and 33 horses.

Left: The Silcock family pictued in a newspaper article announcing the plans for their new amusement centre - Funland. Below: Lord Fearn of Southport and Herbert and Jane Silcock officially open Funland in 1988.

The flagship ride was built over a century ago by Savages, of Kings Lynn. Now based on the forecourt of Funland and Southport Pier, the ride was bought by Silcocks in 1989 and took three years to restore. The restored ride made its debut at the Shirdley Show, St Helens. Among the carousel's horses and cockerels still remain many of the original ones carved by Britain's greatest ever fairground carver, Arthur Anderson, of Bristol.

And as for their names – well each is named after members of the Silcock family and their friends.

Top and left: Silcock's Flavours ice cream and coffee bar and Embassy Restaurant.
Below: Funland, the gateway to Southport Pier.

R.W. Almond - Building a Reputation

R.W. Almond Builders Merchants Ltd, based at 104, Stephensons Way Industrial Estate, Formby, is the local independent family builders' merchants. For over a quarter of a century the firm has been supplying a huge variety of product lines for both trade and DIY, including brick, timber and plasterboard, materials and tools for plumbing, drainage, heating, landscaping, flagging, decorating and ironmongery.

Those visiting the firm's shop can view decorative paving from Bradstone, Marshalls, Plaspave and Lakeland. Huge quantities of natural stone paving in a variety of colours at a very competitive price are also displayed. Helpful staff offer specialist product knowledge and can advise on the correct products and materials for every project from start to finish.

A delivery service is available, with three HGVs and a crane off-loading service available for delivery around the North West, six days a week

Founder of the business was Reginald William Almond who was born in Sefton in 1931. The Almond family were farmers. Reginald's family farmed both dairy and arable at Buckley Hill Farm, Sefton. During the Second World War the family farm covered around 300 acres.

*Top: Founder, Reginald William Almond. **Above:** Young Reg pictured in 1934. **Below:** Buckley Hill Farm, Sefton, where Reg grew up and where he started the business from.*

In due course Reg and Joan would go on to have six children, four of whom are involved in the family business today, whilst the other two became respectively a teacher and a nurse.

George Cameron had founded Camerons of Crosby garage in 1933, selling and servicing Morris, Wolseley and MG cars.

Whilst developing his own plant-hire business in the 1960s Reg was asked by his father-in-law to also help with the running of Camerons of Crosby – a useful way of honing and enhancing his mechanical skills and knowledge.

Reg was educated at Merchants Taylors Boys School and left in 1948 to help on the farm. A lifetime career in farming may have been anticipated by young Reg, but events would intervene - Lord Sefton, the family's landlord, sold all the land for building development. It would be many long decades before Reg would work on a farm again. As a consequence of losing the family farm Reg started a new business with his father called W.R. Almond. The firm constructed playing fields for the schools and houses which had been built on the farm land.

Reg would eventually marry Joan, the daughter of George and Marge Cameron.

Though house building and civil engineering works had been in the doldrums in the post war years, by the 1960s a boom had begun which would be sustained for over a decade. Reg Almond's business would share the dividend of that boom period characterised as the 'Swinging Sixties'.

Top left: Reg (5th left) and R.W. Almond staff pictured in 1975. *Left and above left:* Part of the R.W. Almond fleet and machinery in the 1970s.

carried out around the country, including clearing out old colliery spoil tips at Oswestry, Wigan, Preston and Bolton and landscaping the areas for leisure use, including creating a golf course in London.

Eldest son Richard joined the company from school, and son-in-law Patrick Pettican joined Reg as Contracts Manager, along with long-serving employee John Ellison who would in time become a director of the company.

It was in a corner of the site at Formby that the Builders Merchants started out as a very small garden centre selling sheds, greenhouses, plants and decorative products.

In 1970 Reg bought land at Stephensons Way, Formby, and moved the contracting business there, the current site of Homebase. Despite more difficult economic times for the country as a whole in the 1970s the company, now called R.W. Almond & Co Ltd, prospered and employed around forty people. Major earth-moving contracts were

On finishing his education Reg's second son David expressed an interest in expanding the garden centre and he, together with eldest daughter Susan and youngest son Chris, became responsible for the development of the Builders Merchants.

Top left: *In the top left of this picture from 1970 is the old R.W. Almond pemises. Top right is the old Tom England Volkswagen site which was purchased by Almond's in the mid-1980s and is now home to R.W. Almond's Builders Merchants. Also of interest in the foreground is the old Woodward Garage.* **Above:** *Filling in work at Liverpool docks.* **Left:** *R.W. Almond plant on site at the Merchant Taylors School for the installation of a new swimming pool.*

Meanwhile, the plant side of the family enterprise continued at Netherton - local work included the development of the marine promenade at Crosby Baths, ground works for the original pool at Merchant Taylors Boys School, preparation of parts of the Liverpool Garden Festival Site and the reclamation of the Rimrose Valley site into a Country Park.

The timing was perfect. Though garden centres and DIY centres had been around for some time it was not until the 1980s that they truly began to come into their own. Increasing prosperity, more leisure time, car ownership and an expanding interest in the 'quality of life' not only made it possible for increasing

numbers of homeowners to travel to such out-of-town locations, but also gave them the means, motive and opportunity to take advantage of the products on offer. In subsequent years popular home and garden makeover programmes on television would fuel interest even further.

Around 1985 the business moved again when the site at Formby was sold to Peerless Discount D.I.Y.. Land was now purchased at Heysham Road, Netherton, for the plant hire side of the business, and what was until then a Volkswagen site was purchased at Stephensons Way. It is here that today's successful Builders Merchants has been developed over the last three decades, providing the people of Formby and surrounding area with all their building requirements.

This page: R.W. Almond & Co. Contracting Ltd's Heysham Road, Netherton site (top) and members of the Netherton team: Patrick Pettican - Managing Director (above far left); John Ellison - Director, who has been with the company since 1975 (above centre); Richard Almond - Director (above); Alan Dolbear - Machine Operator, who joined the company in 1976 (left); Carole Barnes - Admin (right); Shaun Spence - MOT Fitter (below); and Steve Parry - Workshop Fitter (below right).

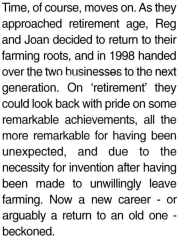

Time, of course, moves on. As they approached retirement age, Reg and Joan decided to return to their farming roots, and in 1998 handed over the two businesses to the next generation. On 'retirement' they could look back with pride on some remarkable achievements, all the more remarkable for having been unexpected, and due to the necessity for invention after having been made to unwillingly leave farming. Now a new career - or arguably a return to an old one - beckoned.

Reg and Joan moved to the Lake District to operate a working sheep farm at Isel, near Cockermouth, with 450 sheep; outbuildings there have been developed into superior self-catering holiday cottages, part of Irton House Farm, expressly designed for guests with limited mobility, especially wheelchair users.

The company was also involved in reclaiming and filling in various docks in Liverpool for the Mersey Docks and Harbour Board, and works with the National Trust at Formby Point and for Sefton Council relocating Arthur Gormley`s 'Iron Men' on Crosby Beach.

Top left: Directors Dave and Chris Almond. ***Below left:*** Susan Pettican - Director (left) and Lin Almond - Admin (right). ***Bottom left:*** Wagon drivers, l-r: Mike Birnie, Des Pope, who has been with the company for 27 years, and Neil Larsen. ***Bottom centre:*** L-r: John Charnock - Assistant Manager, Colin Molloy - Yard Manager and Stephen Tinsley - Counter Assistant. ***Bottom, second right:*** Adam Dawes - Yard Assistant. ***Bottom right:*** Iveneusz 'Eric' Sadowski - Yard Assistant (bottom, second left). ***Below:*** One of the company's delivery vehicles.

Specialising in bulk excavation both on and off site, landscaping (hard and soft), land reclamation and Plant hire, the current customer base includes a majority of the major building and Civil Engineering companies together with local authorities within the surrounding areas.

Reg and Joan's children, David, Susan and Chris, are today backed by some 16 loyal, dependable and dedicated members of staff, many of whom have been with the company for over 25 years, a commendable achievement these days. Together they make up a friendly and knowledgeable team offering unparalleled advice on every kind of building and landscaping project.

Today the company supplies a huge variety of product lines suitable for both trade professionals and self-builders. There is a

brickyard stocked with vast quantities of bricks, blocks and Indian sandstone in various colours. And there are so many other lines; it is a DIY paradise with Polypipe plumbing, fencing, timber, decking, wooden and concrete fence posts, cements, decorative aggregates, plasterboards and plaster, tools, paints, chemicals and industrial workwear.

The list of products seems endless and also includes Velux and Roto windows and rooflights, corrugated roofing, tiling products

and electrical goods. Those stocking up for the summer party season will have no difficulty finding Calor Gas, butane or propane for their barbecues.

Open seven days a week, R.W. Almond Builders Merchants Ltd has a well earned reputation for meeting everyone's building needs. A family firm with family values. it aims to continue to develop over the coming years, and to maintain and enhance the high standards which have ensured its growth since the company was founded.

Left: A view inside R.W. Almonds Builders Merchants shop. *Above:* The building products yard and facility. *Below left: Reg at home in Isel, near Cockermouth. Below:* Reg and Joan Almond, 2011.

Demeva Ltd
Specialists in Temperature Controlled Environments

I n the 21st century refrigeration is everywhere. In homes, shops, supermarkets and warehouses, lorries and ships. It wasn't always like that. Older readers will recall the days when a fridge was a rare thing to find in one's home. Some readers may even recall butchers and fishmongers taking delivery of large blocks of ice which they placed in ice-boxes to keep their produce cool.

The idea of using ice to keep food fresh or invigorating isn't new. Saladin famously sent Richard the Lionheart iced-sherbet, made using ice carried by mounted couriers all the way from distant mountain tops down to the heat of Palestine.

In 1626 Sir Francis Bacon created the world's first frozen chicken by stuffing it with snow to see if it would be kept fresh. The chicken was indeed preserved. Famously Bacon wasn't: he caught a fatal chill!

In England until relatively modern times ice-houses were a common sight. With thick walls, and often half submerged in the ground, the ice-houses would be filled with ice from frozen ponds in the winter. In summer the slowly melting ice could be taken from the ice-house to be used by those lucky enough to have access to such a summer luxury.

Modern refrigeration units were developed in the 19th century though it would be the 1920s before the first fridges suitable for home use began to appear.

Not until the late 1960s would the majority of British houses contain a fridge. Meanwhile the technology continued to evolve, and with that evolution the use of refrigeration in commercial and industrial settings would expand as rapidly as the domestic market.

Demeva Ltd is a Formby-based operation specialising in all aspects of design and installation of refrigeration and associated insulation and doors for the construction of cold-store, chillstores, blast freezers and food processing rooms.

The company also specialises in the installation of fully-ducted air-conditioning, split and variable volume systems, food display counters, insulated panels and doors – including repairs and maintenance contracts.

Top left and top right: *Founders, Alan Dempsey (top left) and Eric Evans.* ***Left:*** *Demeva's Stephenson Way premises.* ***Above:*** *Paul Crolley who joined Demeva in 1987 pictured in his earlier years with the company.*

The business was started in November 1985, by Alan Dempsey and Eric Evans in an office at the rear of Alan's garage. Eric and Alan combined their wealth of experience in refrigeration – and their names – to create a company which is now a market leader, widely respected by others in the industry, as well as by their large client base.

Eric looked after sales and Alan, and his wife Angela, looked after everything else between them; contracting, design, drawings, costing, typing, invoices and wages.

They bought the site in Stephenson Way, Formby, in 1986 and built the current factory there in 1988.

Paul Crolley joined Demeva in 1987 as an apprentice refrigeration engineer and he is set to take over as Managing Director in January 2012.

Historically the firm began life as Refrigeration Engineers, but the founders realised in 1988 that half of their turnover was going to insulation sub-contractors, so in order to get more control of the finances and the contracts they started an insulation business in 1988, and today it is one of the few such companies to have both disciplines in-house.

Subsequently they were asked more and more to get involved in projects at earlier stages and so began to offer a complete package, looking after design, planning, building regulation and CDM (Health and Safety).

The ability to provide all the services associated with construction, insulation and refrigeration projects in-house uniquely allows the company to provide a greater degree of efficiency, co-ordination and accountability, which is reflected in savings for its customers in both time and money.

Much of Demeva's progress is down to a remarkably experienced workforce. Karen Bates - Office Manager, Paul Murphy - Finance Director, George Baddeley - Insulation Manager, and Ian Simister - General Engineering Manager, have each worked for the firm for more than twenty years. Others such as George Harrison - Insulation Manager, and Adrian Spencer - Refrigeration Manager, are not far behind them. In fact around half of the staff at Demeva have over 10 years' service with the firm.

Top left: Alan Dempsey pictured in the 1980s. Top right: Karen Bates, Office Manager, who has been with the company for 22 years. Left: George Baddeley pictured on the Christmas Carol Wagon for The Rotary Club of Formby. Below: Paul Crolley, 2011.

From a modest start the company is a multi-million pound business occupying 24,000 sq ft purpose-built premises. Demeva handles turnkey operations and is frequently appointed as main contractors. Its ability to provide all services associated with refrigeration and insulation in-house is unmatched.

Alan Dempsey still heads the business and benefits by the team of dedicated staff able to call on a vast amount of knowledge and experience to tackle any project successfully. The company also has a team of mobile service engineers, equipped with the latest telecommunication equipment and on call 24 hours a day, 365 days a year for emergency response. They offer a repair service for insulated doors and damaged insulation panels.

Demeva uses the highest quality plant and equipment, but also occasionally offers the option of using re-manufactured plant to keep costs to a minimum, on a supply only, or supply and install basis. The design team at Demeva is equipped with state-of-the-art computer aided design facilities. This supports the engineers and gives customers the confidence of knowing that their project is being handled by professionals at every stage.

The company marked its 25th anniversary in 2010 by completing a multi-million pound temperature-controlled factory on the Wirral. The project was for Tulip Foods, in Bromborough, where the client's existing 34,000 sq mtr facility had been idle for almost a year.

An extremely tight programme of works, due to planning and construction constraints, was made doubly challenging by the extreme winter conditions. Despite this Demeva as principal contractor handed over the new factory on time and within budget.

New building consisted of a 'Goods in' extension, a 'Goods Out' extension and a new Production Hall and Frozen Storage area.

The new Production Hall runs the full length of the building. At 17,000 sq mtrs it incorporates a Holding Freezer and Spiral Freezer together with the new production area.

The entire project added 1,050 kw of refrigeration to the existing plant. The new plant incorporates the latest energy saving features to assist in enhancing the site's green credentials.

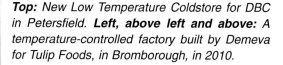

*Top: New Low Temperature Coldstore for DBC in Petersfield. **Left, above left and above:** A temperature-controlled factory built by Demeva for Tulip Foods, in Bromborough, in 2010.*

As well as being responsible for the design, civil works, steelwork and cladding Demeva's contract also included refrigeration, insulation, doors, electrical services, lighting specialist flooring, stainless steel kerb, drains, plumbing and alterations to all the offices.

Demeva's skills base has taken it outside the UK to complete projects in some of the most challenging places in the world, including a number of installations at a large dairy facility in Lagos, Nigeria, as well as places closer to home such as Ireland and Poland. Clients include the NHS, Local Authorities the Police, HJ Heinz, Northern Foods, Langdons, DBC, Tulip Foods and many more.

George Baddeley looked after the structural alterations. A local firm, Formby Car Electrics, installed the new music system.

In 1998 Demeva was involved with some charity work for Zoe's Place Children's Hospice in Liverpool and asked if the firm could look at the possibility of refrigerating a cot/bed so that bereaved parents could spend more time with their child. They did it, and it worked. They then made another at Zoe's Place in Middlesbrough. The design changed to utilising the standard NHS nursery trolley and finally to the current design with Demeva supplying the complete cot. The firm has since made over 40 cots including one for Sydney, New South Wales, Australia.

Demeva also take a keen interest in the local area and in 1989 they sponsored the kit for the football team at Holy Trinity Primary School. Coincidentally twenty years later, Daniel Blake, as Captain of Formby Dons football team, asked if Demeva would sponsor their kit. According to Daniel 'Our kit was almost four years old and falling to bits but we couldn't afford new ones. I wrote to almost 100 businesses in Formby and was delighted when Alan Dempsey gave me a call to say he wanted to sponsor us. We then realised he had sponsored my football team when I was about seven or eight. It's astonishing he's still helping Formby's teams out in this way."

After more than a quarter of a century in business Demeva Ltd has truly earned its place as one of the UK's leading construction, insulation and refrigeration specialists.

*Top left: A storage systems built and maintained by Demeva. **Above:** A Demeva food processing facility. **Centre, both pictures:** Ian Simister, General Engineering Manager, (left) and Paul Murphy, Finance Director, who have both worked for Demeva for 22 years. **Below and below left:** Alan Dempsey presents Captain of Formby Dons football team, Daniel Blake, with their new kit sponsored by Demeva (below) and Alan pictured with Holy Trinity Primary School who they sponsored in the 1980s and who, coincidentally, Daniel Blake (circled) played for.*

Since 1993 Demeva has looked after the Christmas Carol Wagon for The Rotary Club of Formby, rebuilding the original caravan they were using until 1998 when Alan was President of the Rotary Club. Alan and Paul Crolley redesigned the Carol Wagon using a milk float acquired from one of their customers. Paul installed all of the electrical and mechanical changes and

Southport's Family Jewellers

Connard & Son Ltd - The Oldest Family Firm on Lord Street

By the last quarter of the nineteenth century Lord Street was widely regarded as not only one of the most fashionable thoroughfares in the country but also one of the most beautiful. The street boasted many fine and varied shops on one side, faced by impressive civic buildings and gardens. This vibrant and progressive new boulevard must have certainly impressed young Walter Connard, the eldest son of a local builder, who dreamed of opening a jewellery business in the centre of the town.

Walter, the eldest of seven sons, was born in 1859 and was educated at Christ Church School. On leaving school he was apprenticed to a firm of architects, but still dreamed of a career as a jeweller. When he was just 20 his father died leaving him to take charge of the family building business. Indeed the 1881 census describes him as a 'master bricklayer' employing no less than 48 men. But by the year 1883 he had achieved his childhood ambition and opened a jewellery shop near the end of what was then the business section of Lord Street. In those early days the building, which occupied the site of the present shop, was just single storey with a garden running down to the road. Always enterprising and with much foresight, Walter subsequently purchased the land and built the Masonic Buildings, which was the first large building north of Nevill Street. In fact the building boasted a wider

verandah than any previously and was the first to be fitted with curved glass – which later became a characteristic feature and standard for Lord Street. In partnership with his brother Arthur this new venture soon prospered and laid the foundations for one of Southport's best known businesses which is now celebrating its fourth generation as a family firm in the very heart of the town.

Top left: Walter Connard (1859-1946) pictured when he was also Managing Director of the Palladium, which has now sadly gone, but his Mermaid fountain remains as one of Southport's best known landmarks. Left: Shop front circa 1889 with the present, but repositioned, front door and before Lord Street was re-numbered; number 227 becoming 421. Above: Connards' workshop with young William Porter on the extreme right hand side.

By 1939 Connards Jewellers was a well established firm of over 56 years and, with Walter's son Charles in the business, it was now in its second generation. Charles not only ran the family jewellers but was also an inspector in the Southport Special Constabulary and during the war was in charge of the town's Royal Observer Corps. At this time the jewellery business took on a secondary importance. There were a number of occasions when the shop doorway was barricaded with sand bags, not because of hostilities but to keep the water out when Lord Street regularly flooded! However, the declaration of war had brought with it certain restrictions on jewellery businesses in general. During this period only 9ct gold was allowed and many customers hoped that a new 22ct wedding ring could be found for their daughter – and they were sometimes successful.

Walter Connard's interest and experience in the building trade never left him as by 1912 he had plans passed for altering his Lord Street property and demolishing his Stanley Street property in order to build a Picture Palace. Always a man of vision he had quickly realised that there would be quite a future in live entertainment and film shows, which were by then extremely popular. The entrance to his proposed new Picture Palace was to have been next door to his jewellers shop. But these ambitious plans were altered when a customer, Sir Leonard Williamson, learned what he was planning and decided to join him in building a much larger and impressive Picture Palace, *The Palladium*, which opened in 1914. This occupied the site where Sainsbury's supermarket now stands.

The Palladium was a huge success and Walter remained as its Managing Director for the first eight years, while still running his jewellery business. Southport Council was anxious to acquire the land in front of the picture palace for their expanding public gardens scheme, so they entered into negotiations with Walter. As part of the final deal, the Council was to build a fountain – but to Walter's designs, in front of his Palladium. This was to be a centrepiece in the formal gardens and the resulting 'mermaid fountain' is now one of Southport's best known landmarks.

Top: *Interior view of the shop (circa 1889) with gas lighting and the same Honduras mahogany display cabinets, counter cases and chairs. Today the shop's interior fittings remain largely unchanged, except for modern electric lighting.* ***Left:*** *Lord Street's famous Mermaid fountain.* ***Above:*** *The Palladium on Lord Street, now replaced by Sainsbury's supermarket.*

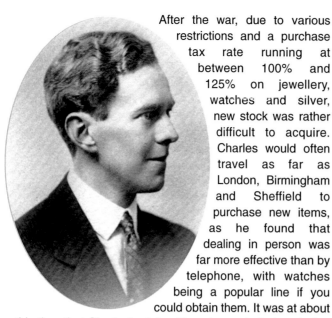

After the war, due to various restrictions and a purchase tax rate running at between 100% and 125% on jewellery, watches and silver, new stock was rather difficult to acquire. Charles would often travel as far as London, Birmingham and Sheffield to purchase new items, as he found that dealing in person was far more effective than by telephone, with watches being a popular line if you could obtain them. It was at about this time that Charles's sister, Georgiana, started analysing the sales and continued to do so until she reached the grand old age of 91 years – without ever relying on a calculator!

In 1966 Charles's son, Martin, joined the family firm as the third generation. Martin's father always stressed that a business should never rest on its laurels, no matter how established, but should be innovative and try out new ideas whilst keeping the values of old fashioned courtesy, respect and customer service ever in the forefront. These ideals have been the very hallmark of Connards Jewellers to this day.

Martin's wife Janet now began taking a more active part in running the business, as their children, Elizabeth and Andrew, were growing older. This was in much the same way as Charles Connard's wife Helen had done many years earlier. 2003 saw yet another generation of the family joining the firm as Andrew decided to continue the tradition. Andrew has already made his mark on the

business through his love of watches and clocks, expanding this side of the business considerably. Andrew also brought the business into the computer age. One of the endearing features of Connards Jewellers has always been the delightfully old-fashioned interior of the shop with its ticking clocks and Victorian mahogany glass display cases. Yet still the old world charm and ambience remains. Every jeweller needs a specialisation that will set them apart and Connards' expertise is coloured gems. Martin is indeed a Fellow of the Gemmological Association of Great Britain and has a vast knowledge of gemstones of all types.

Successful retail businesses aren't just good buildings and quality merchandise but are moulded by the people who run them and the customers they deal with. A firm as old as Connards has seen many personalities come and go over the last 128 years, some joining as mere boys and staying well after retirement age. One such memorable character was William Porter (always called 'Arthur' to avoid confusion with another William on the staff) who started work as an apprentice in 1899. In those days Connards not only sold fine jewellery and silverware but had a small manufacturing and repair workshop within their Lord Street premises. William was just 13 years of age when he started work and was pleased to stay until he was 70! Sound testimony to a happy working environment, if ever there was one. One of William's early tasks was to go to various customers' homes on the same day each week to wind and regulate their clocks, a service for which they would be charged a guinea a year!

The firm's logo of a sailing galleon on the high seas is quite an apt image for a family with a record of success in uncharted waters as in 2008 Martin's daughter

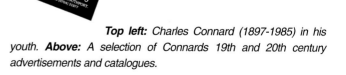

Top left: Charles Connard (1897-1985) in his youth. *Above:* A selection of Connards 19th and 20th century advertisements and catalogues.

Elizabeth, a Cordon Bleu trained patisserie chef, opened a patisserie and wedding cake business, Lilibets of Paris, in Stanley Street, directly behind Connards' Lord Street jewellers shop. Paradoxically, the reputation of Elizabeth's baking skills has even resulted in a wedding cake order from France! As a family the Connards feel honoured by the number of people who frequently travel considerable distances especially to visit their shop, for as with any retail jewellers, it is only through the loyalty of customers both old and new that the business can exist in the first place.

oldest family firm, which now spans three centuries, as a fifth generation Connard has just made his debut in the shop – even though he's only a few weeks old! Time only can tell if baby Matthew Connard, Martin's young grandson, will continue in the proud family tradition of quality and service which his great, great grandfather began all those years ago.

Left: Interior view of the shop in Centenary Year (1983) with Martin, Helen, Charles and team. ***Above:*** The present day Connards team, ensuring there is always a warm welcome. ***Below:*** The present day Connards shop front in marble and bronze.

Those who have not yet visited the shop can be assured a very warm welcome and a chance to judge for themselves the range and quality of the items on offer and customer satisfaction is, and always has been, an overriding priority.

It's clear that this family can rightly claim to be true 'Sandgrounders' in every way as the grandmother of the business's founder, Walter Connard, was actually born in a cottage on the site of the present Atkinson Art Gallery on Lord Street. This would have been only a few years after the very founding of the town itself in 1792! The future certainly looks bright for Lord Street's

C.H. Latham - THE Baker

When Chris first started the business in 1967 a small white loaf cost just one shilling (5p). Today the cost of a similar loaf may have changed dramatically, but something which hasn't changed down the years is the quality which the firm is proud to have maintained and enhanced.

Before setting himself up in business Chris had previously served his time as an apprentice at Laces Bakery in Wigan, gaining his City & Guilds qualifications in Bread Making, Confectionery and Cake Decoration at Bolton Technical College.

At Oak Street, Chris started baking on his own, with a part-time sales assistant working in the shop in the mornings. Chris worked in the shop in the afternoons. Baking in the mornings, serving in the shop in the afternoons made for long days.

In the early days everything was made by hand, the only equipment was the mixer that made all the bread, and cakes, and a coke-fired double-deck oven that had to be fired up each afternoon to heat up ready for the early morning bread baking. As the day progressed and the oven temperature began to fall then the cakes could be baked.

There is surely no more mouthwatering smell than the scent of freshly baked bread floating in the air. And the Southport area is particularly blessed.

C.H.Latham The Baker Ltd was founded by Chris Latham when at the age of just 21 he took over the bakery and shop in Oak Street previously owned by Walmsley and Haydock.

Top left: Oak Street in 1967. **Left and above:** C.H. Latham's Crossens (left) and Birkdale shops.

If the wind got up during the night, Chris, who lived above the shop, would have to get up and close the flue vents otherwise the fire would burn away and the oven be too hot to bake bread in.

One night in the early days there was a torrential storm and when Chris got up the yard was flooded, the ash pit to the oven filled up with water and the fire had gone out. The bakery was standing in two inches of water.

Chris had to start cleaning up and relight the fire after bailing out the fire pit. The bread was late that day!

Chris ran the business as Managing Director while his wife Ann dealt with all the cashing-up of the tills as well as overseeing the shop.

In 1969 they took on their second shop at the corner of Pool Lane, Crossens. After two years they moved to larger premises in the centre of the village. Following greater success and a growing customer base more premises were added. In 1989 they acquired the Roe Lane shop in Churchtown by the library at Lane Ends, and branched out into wholesale supplies to restaurants, hotels and other shops.

When the Birkdale shop was opened in 1999, it made the business the largest retail baker in Southport.

The flour was bought from H&R Ainscough, in Burscough, for the first 20 years in business until that firm was taken over by Allied Mills and the milling transferred to Liverpool.

Chris has always believed in freshness and quality. All the company's goods have always been baked and sold on the same day, using only quality ingredients.

In 2006, Chris decided to open a Cake Studio above the Roe Lane Shop. This has proved a great success, providing delicious Wedding Cakes and Celebration Cakes for every occasion, hand decorated to the personal requirements of the customer.

The company has become widely known for all its products, but particularly its pies – being a Wigan lad Chris was weaned on pies. If anyone is asked if they know 'Lathams' they always mention the firm's "tasty pies". But its not just pies that have made the firm's name: other specialities are its Eccles cakes and its famous 'Continentals' which are fruited flat bread with a layer of macaroon inside, covered with nuts and topped with water icing.

Today, the company employs 53 staff in the bakery and in its four shops. There are plans to open another six shops over the next few years, each keeping the same ethos that has been the 'secret' of business growth over the last five decades.

Chris Latham still runs the business as its Managing Director; his wife Ann, is now retired.

Top left and above: C.H. Latham's Churchtown shop. **Far left:** An example of the beautiful hand decorated celebration cakes made by C.H. Latham, available for any occasion. **Left:** Mouthwatering Latham products. **Below:** C.H. Latham's Oak Street head office premises, 2011.

Hodge Halsall LLP

A Professional Service Provided In a Friendly and Approachable Manner

The Law is a mystery to most of us. Yet sooner or later we may require the help of a legal expert. Wills, a divorce, business contracts all require a degree of specialist knowledge.

Happily we can rely on solicitors to help us out. And one of the longest established firm of solicitors in Southport is Hodge Halsall LLP.

The firm's lawyers each specialise in their individual practice fields allowing them to provide in-depth advice in several legal areas. They aim to provide innovative business and personal solutions for clients, to work with and support them.

Representation in courts, tribunals and other legal forums is provided on a daily basis in civil, employment and family proceedings. A full range of non-contentious services is also provided, including conveyancing, elder law, wills, probate and trust work.

A client-focused package of commercial services, including business acquisitions and start-ups, commercial property, people issues, dispute resolution and regulatory issues is available to businesses.

But who are Hodge Halsall?

Wilmot Hodge was born in Southport on 11 December, 1867. His brother, Reginald Hodge, also a native of the town, was born on 18 December, 1876.

Wilmot was admitted as a solicitor in 1889 and was eventually joined by Reginald (who qualified in 1899) to form the law firm W & R Hodge.

Wilmot was involved in an early prosecution for a driving offence in 1901, the year in which the first motor insurance policy was underwritten by Lloyds.

The firm moved to its current premises at 18, Hoghton Street, Southport, in 1907 and has remained there ever since.

The Hodge brothers were joined by Robert Halsall, originally as an articled clerk in 1907, and subsequently as a partner, to form W & R Hodge & Halsall. Robert Halsall's father had to pay Wilmot Hodge the sum of £100 (equivalent to approximately £9,000 today) to allow his son to be articled to Wilmot Hodge. This was standard practice at the time and for many years hence.

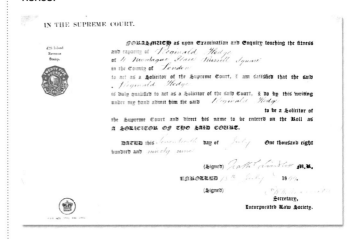

Wilfred Hodge fought in World War I as a volunteer and received a letter of thanks for his service from the King signed by the Secretary of State for War – Winston Churchill.

Founder of the firm, Wilmot Hodge, died on 9 October, 1942, but had been pre-deceased by his brother Reginald who died on 11 November, 1939.

Following the retirement of Wilmot and Reginald Hodge, Cuthbert Rudyard Halsall joined Robert Halsall. Cuthbert subsequently continued in practice as the sole partner. His practice seems to

Top left: *Wilmot Hodge.* **Above:** *Reginald Hodge's admittance to act as a solicitor for the Supreme Court, dated July 1899.* **Left:** *The letter of thanks received by Wilfred Hodge, signed by Winston Churchill.*

Carter Hodge had a number of offices with premises in Southport, Birkdale, Ainsdale, Formby, St Helens, Heswall, Liverpool and Chester. The firm was at the forefront of promoting quality standards within solicitors firms throughout the 1990s. It was in the first wave of firms to achieve a legal aid franchise, and was one of the first firms in the country to be awarded both the Law Society's practice management standard, Lexcel, and the Investors in People standard – quality marks which the firm retains to this day.

In 2005 Carter Hodge merged with Maxwell Entwistle & Byrne to create Maxwell Hodge but in 2007 partners Mark Robinson, Gordon Hatton and Judith Bond separated the Southport and Ainsdale offices away from Maxwell Hodge to form the current firm of Hodge Halsall LLP.

have thrived as can be seen by the number of staff in the photograph above dating from September 1947, taken to the rear of 18 Hoghton Street.

Cuthbert Halsall retired from the firm on 30 April, 1960. The practice, however, continued to thrive with an increasing number of partners, one of whom, David Byard, joined the firm as a solicitor in 1976 on the princely annual salary of £2,250. David retired in 2005. W & R Hodge & Halsall were ahead of their time in employing staff usually deemed as past retirement age. The combined age of their two office juniors in the 1970s was 160 years!

W & R Hodge & Halsall merged with another Southport firm, Russell & Sutton, on 1 January 1985, to create the snappily titled Hodge, Halsall, Russell & Sutton. Solicitor Gordon Hatton was a partner in Russell & Sutton at the time, and remains a partner today in Hodge Halsall LLP.

In 1989 Hodge, Halsall, Russell & Sutton merged with Liverpool and Ainsdale firm Cliff Carter & Co to create Carter Hodge. Mark Robinson, a partner in Cliff Carter & Co, is now Managing Partner of Hodge Halsall LLP.

Now offering a broad range of legal services to both commercial organisations and individuals from all over the country, Hodge Halsall remains as committed to its roots in Southport as the Hodge brothers were back in the days when they established the firm.

Top left and above: *Staff and partners pictured in 1947 (top left) and 1998 (above).* **Below:** *Hodge Halsall's Hoghton Street premises, 2011.*

Millars Ark Toys Ltd

Importers and Distributors

Millars Ark Toys Ltd is a family firm which has been supplying major attractions and national charities, both at home and abroad, for over half a century. The company was founded by Bryan Millar in 1959. The idea for the business came to Bryan when, as a tourist in Edinburgh, he couldn't find a specific souvenir. Realising there was a gap in the market he decided to do something about it.

Bryan secured an order for 500 cloth pennants and built the company up from there, selling pennants and key rings then branching out into plastic and soft toys to keep up with the market demand.

Initially Bryan worked from home before sharing an office with his father in Southport's Wayfarers Arcade on Lord Street.

Much of Bryan's time was spent on the road, buying from wholesalers, showing samples and visiting perspective clients.

By 1986 Bryan and his part time secretary were struggling with their workload.

Bryan now brought his son, Steven, into the business, bringing with him experience gained whilst

Top left: Founder, Bryan Millar. **Below:** The company's exhibition stand at the Blackpool International Gift Fair in 1971. **Above right:** A recent exhibition stand at Birmingham NEC trade fair.

Today, the company imports from many sites in the Far East such as Hong Kong, China, Indonesia, Vietnam and Taiwan, and exports to customers all around the world, including Dubai, Japan, Australia and even the Falkland Islands, often shipping directly from the manufacturer to the client. The firm also has agents in Spain and Portugal.

Throughout Britain one only need to visit any major tourist attraction to see Ark Toys products, and many hospices and charities use the firm's products in their fundraising.

Steven Millar has recently accepted an invitation to join the Equitoy Council, which involves him advising and giving opinions or various issues surrounding the manufacturing and selling of toys, including safety, import controls and EU legislation.

taking a business studies course. The firm was working out of offices on Maple Street.

This was when the company started selling plush toys and animal themed gifts to zoos and safari parks, hence the name 'Ark' Toys. The also started importing directly from manufacturers.

In the early 1990s the company moved into a small unit on a newly-built industrial estate, the Enterprise Business Park in Russell Road, taking 500 sq. ft. Steven then concentrated on sourcing goods from the Far East, and, keeping with family tradition, brought in his sister-in-law Tracy to focus on sales, leaving Bryan and his secretary Mary to look after the accounts.

The company soon expanded into direct importing and distribution. It took more and more warehouse space to accommodate the constantly expanding range necessary to meet the demands of its many varied customers, and it now employed 10 full time staff. Today, the offices and warehouse take up 80% of the A. K. Business Park, also on Russell Road.

In 1999, one of Britain's largest holiday providers placed an order for bespoke items to sell at all its sites. The value of the order was half a million pounds, by far the biggest order the company had ever had. The huge order allowed the company to move forward with bespoke items and invest more in the future.

Sadly, company founder Bryan Millar died in 2002. The baton now passed to his son Steven. In 2009 the company's 50th anniversary was celebrated with a ball in aid of Southport's Queenscourt Hospice where Bryan Millar had passed away.

Top left and above: *Millars Ark Toys' showroom, Russell Road, Southport.* ***Below:*** *Steven Millar (front centre) and staff at the company's 50th Anniversary Ball, in 2009, in aid of Southport's Queenscourt Hospice.*

David Halsall Sons & Daughter - A Real Family Firm

Long ago some of us could move home with just a handcart to carry all our worldly possessions. These days we usually need the help of experts. When it comes to moving David Halsall Sons & Daughter Ltd understands that moving home or business premises can be one of the most stressful tasks in life: that's why the firm aims to provide a simple and straightforward service second to none. The local company operates a fleet of vehicles ranging from the standard Transit van to 17 tonne furniture van - enabling it to cater for any size of removals.

The firm's services range from local house and commercial removals, to national moves, partload and packing. The company also provides bespoke and specialist removals services.

As the name implies, David Halsall Sons & Daughter Removals Ltd is a family-run business. Based in Virginia Street, Southport, the firm has been providing removals and storage services in Southport, throughout Merseyside, the North West and nationally since 1977.

Over the years the firm has built a reputation for quality and reliability, so much so that a much of its business now comes from recommendations. Clients range from Councils, the NHS, schools and Housing Associations to well-known national companies, and, of course, also include everyone moving house.

Until he founded the business David Halsall had worked as a warehouseman. Today the firm employs ten staff. Back in 1977, however, the removals firm comprised just David, helped as and when by his father.

David's father helped in any way he could, not least looking after the office and doing estimates, freeing up David to do the actual removals in his Commer Luton van.

As the business grew David's mother, and later his wife, Lynne, began to help.

The business started life running from David's home in Glen Park Drive, Southport, before moving to Tithebarn Road, Southport. In 1987 the firm moved again, this time to 270 Liverpool Road.

In later years both of David and Lynne's sons, Peter and James, joined the business as removal men and Emma their daughter in the office.

In 2010 the firm moved to the Virginia Mews Business Centre in Virginia Street. It was there that a second business enterprise was formed, Southport Storage Solutions Ltd run by David's son Peter and daughter Emma.

Top left: *Founder, David Halsall.* ***Left:*** *On a job to the Shetlands in 1992.* ***Above and inset:*** *Lynne Halsall with son Peter and pictured inset is daughter Emma in the mid-1980s.*

David Halsall, Sons & Daughter Ltd's clients can be confident that staff members offer a first-class value for money removal and storage service. David added: "We have pleasure in offering an estimate without obligation, based on the size of the home. Our company always supplies an accurate arrival time for the removals to commence. This is previously agreed between the client and David Halsall Sons & Daughter. Our hard-earned reputation is one of utmost reliability, our aim is to be true to our word; nor do we add pressure to our clients, our objective is always to relieve pressure, not cause it."

Today, as well as its founder David Halsall, his two sons, daughter, son-in-law and daughter-in-law are all involved in the family business

Southport Storage Solutions provides a full range of professional removals and storage services for home and business.

Despite the inevitable problems associated with periodic economic recessions the business has weathered all storms. The firm has overseen the removals of a wide and disparate client-base requiring office, commercial property and household removals. Specialised packing materials for all purposes are offered. Additionally the company supplies purpose-built storage, heat containerised and general storage facilities along with an expert clearance service, locally or nationwide.

Top left: David Halsall (right) pictured with their longest serving employee Peter Huyton who joined the company in 1988. **Above:** Inside Southport Storage Solutions Managed by Peter and Emma Halsall. **Below:** David and daughter Emma in 2011.

Noted for having an excellent team who all play their part, the company is proud of the quality and longevity of service of its staff. In David Halsall's words: "Our staff are local and long-serving. All of the David Halsall Sons & Daughter staff are pleasant, polite, trustworthy and willing to take on any removal or storage task in order to please our clients – even those needs outside of the original request."

David goes on: "When dealing with the property of the client, it is always treated as if it was our own. We believe that is why we are such a long-established removal and storage firm, respected and well renowned throughout Formby, Southport and the Merseyside area in general."

Cockshott Peck Lewis - Help with the Law

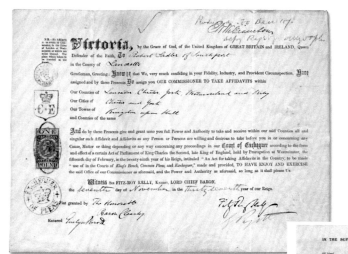

The firm is the result of a number of amalgamations over a long period of years, with the origins of three of the predecessor firms stretching back more than a century.

One of the predecessors, Cockshott Rayner & Loy, was derived from a main office in Preston known as Buck and Dixon. Another was derived from the Ormskirk firm of Parr and Sadler, and a third from a firm in Wigan called Mayhew Son & Peck. These three firms had small branch offices in Southport at a time when Southport was developing in the Victorian era.

Buck & Dixon's opened an office in Southport in the 1860s. Parr & Sadler of Ormskirk had a branch in Southport at 149, Lord Street, in 1868, or thereabouts. Mayhew Son & Peck's branch at 30, Hoghton Street was opened in 1876.

Cockshott Peck Lewis is a solicitors' firm of six partners. The main office is at 24, Hoghton Street, with branches in Station Road, Ainsdale, and in Cambridge Road, Churchtown.

Every type of work is undertaken, except Admiralty work such as collisions at sea. When specialist advice is required the firm instructs barristers or 'counsel' in Manchester, Liverpool or London, as necessary.

The work of the practice is divided broadly into two: contentious work, litigation or court proceedings, or potential litigation on the one hand, and non-contentious work on the other. Non-contentious work includes conveyancing, wills, trusts, probate and a host of other matters, including tax planning.

The firms' names changed over the years. Buck and Dixon became Buck Cockshott & Cockshott - later on Cockshott & Rayner and still later Cockshott Rayner & Loy. Mayhew Son & Peck was shortened to Kenneth Peck after the death of that solicitor's brother and father, the former due to being bitten by a rabid dog and dying within twenty-four hours. Parr and Sadler became Parr Sadler Dickinson & Watson subsequently Dickinson Watsons & Parker and later still Watson & Peck. Another firm, started in the 1930s, originally called Walter Sykes became Walter Sykes Lewis & Co. and then, on merger with Watson & Peck, became Peck Lewis Belshaw & Watson.

The late Kenneth Peck was at one time clerk to the Cheshire Lines Extension Railway Company which owned Lord Street

Top left and inset: *A certificate from the Exchequer of Pleas, circa 1874, granting Robert Sadler power and authority to take and receive affidavits on behalf of the Court of Exchequer. Inset is Mason George Cockshott's certificate of qualification to act as a solicitor of the Supreme Court, 1935.* ***Left:*** *Dickinson Watson & Parker partners and staff of 1905.* ***Above right:*** *Gerald Belshaw.*

and the ties with the former head offices were severed, one by one.

The present firm was formed by the amalgamation of Cockshott Rayner & Loy and Peck Lewis Belshaw & Watson in April 1986.

Today's partners are Keith Watson, Graham Holt, Geoff Cottrell, Alistair Ford, Val Hulton and Wendy Tyson, who are assisted by Associate Solicitor Fleur Lawrence.

In 2009 the firm diversified into Estate Agency - 'CPL Properties', which is run from the same three premises.

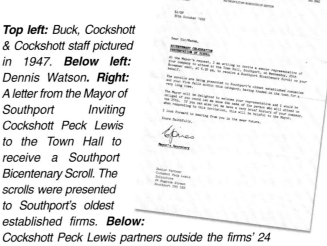

Station - subsequently the Ribble Bus Station, now partly empty and partly Morrisons Supermarket. A former clerk of Kenneth Peck's, William Crompton, remembered the company meetings in the Tower at Lord Street Station and was responsible for writing the dividends out by hand. The late Robert Sadler, of Parr & Sadler, ran for Coroner in the days when they were elected by the Freeholders. He lost to Sir Sam Brighouse, but only after one or both candidates had canvassed the grave space holders who, of course, owned freehold land - the margin was less than twenty votes. One of the late Kenneth Peck's favourite statements (always expressed with a twinkle in the eye) was 'Dust and honesty go together'.

The first female employee was a Miss Levy, whose brother had been office boy until he was called up in 1914. At that time there was an enormous shortage of staff and Mr W.H.Watson asked the office boy if he could recommend anyone: he doubtfully wondered if his sister might possibly do – Miss Levy remained with Dickinsons Watson & Partner and Watson & Peck until the 1970s, witnessing many more changes.

Top left: Buck, Cockshott & Cockshott staff pictured in 1947. Below left: Dennis Watson. Right: A letter from the Mayor of Southport Inviting Cockshott Peck Lewis to the Town Hall to receive a Southport Bicentenary Scroll. The scrolls were presented to Southport's oldest established firms. Below: Cockshott Peck Lewis partners outside the firms' 24 Hoghton Street premises. Back row l-r: Graham Holt, Geoff Cottrell and Alistair Ford, front row l-r: Keith Watson, Val Hulton and Wendy Tyson.

Until the 1939-45 war most documents were prepared by hand on parchment or parchment substitute. Sloping desks and stools once filled the general office at Hoghton Street. Wilfred Schofield, who was also with the firm for fifty years, claimed that the stools were really more comfortable than they looked, and that one got used to leaning against a sloping desk and working with a round ruler.

Over the years the connections with the original parent offices became less important,

K.A. Farr & Co. - Accounting for the Years

Kathryn Farr studied Economics and Social Studies (including Accounting) at Manchester University. She then completed a training contract with one of the 'Big Eight' firms of accountants, Ernst and Young in Liverpool, qualifying as a Chartered Accountant in July 1991.

In August, 1992, Kath Farr joined her father, becoming a partner in April 1994. In May 1996 she qualified as a Member of the Chartered Institute of Taxation, a very highly regarded tax specialist qualification.

Practice Manager Warwick Thomson has over 30 years' experience in accountancy practice. He has been with the company since 1985, responsible for day to day supervision of staff. Warwick also manages his own portfolio of clients consisting of mainly sole traders and partnerships.

Ken Farr, still a consultant, retired in 1995.

Though having grown from a 'one man band' to an organisation with 15 staff the firm prides itself on not only providing the high standard of service established by its founder, but also sound practical assistance, help and advice still given on a personal level.

K.A. Farr & Co, based in Botanic Road, Churchtown, is a family firm of Chartered Accountants. Established in 1972 it was originally based in Shellfield Road, Marshside, in a small extension to Ken Farr's home.

Ken Farr qualified as a Chartered Accountant in 1957, having until then been articled to H.D. Collins, of Westminster Bank Chambers, for five years. After qualifying Ken joined the Merchant Navy, serving mainly aboard the vessel Reina del Mar, until 1961. Ken became a Fellow of the Institute of Chartered Accountants in England and Wales in 1968.

Leaving the Merchant Navy Ken worked briefly in Liverpool, before spending ten years as Financial Director with marble and tile merchants Reed Harris before leaving to establish his own accountancy firm, helped by his wife Elaine. Initially working from home, Ken later took premises in Cambridge Road, Churchtown, as the practice began to grow. In 1981 he moved into the buildings from which the practice operates today. Number 8, Botanic Road would in due course have two extensions added to it, followed by the addition of the next door premises, 6 Botanic Road.

*Above left: Ken and Kath Farr pictured in 1994. **Above:** Practice Manager, Warwick Thomson. **Below:** Kath Farr outside the company's Botanic Road premises.*

The Promenade Care Home for the Elderly

The Promenade Care Home for the Elderly was set up in 1975 to provide long term respite and holiday care. The home has an excellent reputation, achieving RDB five star accreditation, an 'Excellent' rating from the Care Quality Commission and an Investors in People Award.

The long-standing Manager is Sue Astley, who started as a care assistant at the age of 16 in 1979. Many of her team of dedicated staff have worked at the home for well over ten years.

The business was established by Norman and Jean Ibbotson. Today it is supported by their children Michelle, Karen and James. Norman passed away in 2004 his wife Jean retired in 1997.

The home started with ten beds at 10 The Promenade. In the following years numbers 11 and 12 were added.

The home is ideally positioned on the Promenade, overlooking the King's Gardens and just a few steps from the picturesque Lord Street with its many shops and attractions.

Things have changed a good deal since the home first opened; in 1975 few people knew what a residential care home was. It then provided support within a 'guest house' setting, with only a washbasin or large Victorian style washbowl and jug in the rooms.

Set meals were provided each day. That type of care appealed to private paying residents, and was considered quite posh!

Over the years the Promenade Care Home has proactively changed to accommodate modern expectations. The home now offers en-suite rooms, passenger lifts, and fully-trained dedicated staff working to person-centred care plans. There is now a daily choice of menus as well as catering for special dietary requirements. A range of daily activities and trips out in the home's own coach are available for those who wish to take part.

Complimentary massages and manicures are available. The home's facilities also include a visitors lounge, coffee bar, hairdressing salon and the internet. Laptops with Skype facility are available throughout the home, and promoted through activity sessions. A recent Get Connected grant has enabled many of the residents to embrace I.T. and take part in the Promenade Care Home's Facebook page and in their website content. More information on the Promenade Care Home can be seen on their website: www.promenadecarehome.co.uk

Meanwhile the family legacy goes on, with Sammie and Jack, Karen's children, and Michelle's son William showing an interest and often found chatting with residents.

Top: The Promenade Care Home. **Left:** *Residents enjoying a game of basketball in the garden.* **Above:** *A resident relaxing with a complimentary massage and manicure.*

ACKNOWLEDGMENTS

The publishers would like to sincerely thank a number of individuals and organisations

for their help and contribution to this publication.

Sefton Council Library Services

Getty Images - www.gettyimages.co.uk

Press Association - www.pressassociation.com

The late Mr Ted Baxendale

Moving Britain

Ron Hunt - www.southportworld.co.uk